The Official Book

OF THE

Bedlington Terrier

Muriel Lee

PHOTO CREDITS

Contents

About the Author

M uriel Lee has been active in the dog world since 1965, when she purchased her first Old English Sheepdog, and eventually settled on a Scottish Terrier.

She has been a member of the Minneapolis Kennel Club for more than 30 years, also serving as treasurer. She is a member of the Lake Minnetonka Kennel Club and the Scottish Terrier Club of America, for which she has been historian and editor of the STCA yearbooks. She is an AKC-licensed judge of Scottish Terriers and has given frequent talks on the whelping of puppies.

In 1984, she wrote and published her first book, *The Whelping and Rearing of Puppies: A Complete and Practical Guide,* which has been the book of choice for many breeders throughout its numerous printings, and was reissued in 1998. Muriel has also written *The Official Book of the Scottish Terrier* and *The Official Book of the Boston Terrier* for T.F.H. Publications.

Author Muriel Lee with her two champion French Bulldogs.

Introduction

⌒⋎⌒

The Bedlington Terrier is the dog with the look of a lamb and the heart of a lion—a warrior in sheep's clothing. He's been described as clever, tenacious, and resolute; a keen hunter with staying power; a first-class water dog; quiet except when aroused; nimble, quick-witted, and intelligent; charming, gentle, and a terrific companion.

This book will give you an overview of the Bedlington Terrier, from its history to its grooming and breeding. You will read of the pioneers who spent their time and money and gave their hearts to make this a breed that looks unlike any other breed, one that can hunt in the field all day, in addition to being a top-notch family companion. This book discusses the Bedlington Terrier temperament and necessary care. You will find out what will be required of both you and your dog if you want to show your dog or work your dog in obedience. You will learn about the Bedlington Terrier Club of America, what function a breed club serves, and why you may want to belong to the national club or one of the two regional Bedlington Terrier clubs. If you are thinking of breeding your Bedlington, this book will give you some advice to help you decide if you really want to breed your dog or simply enjoy him as a family companion. You will also read the essential facts of every breed history—the top-producing dogs, the great winning dogs, and the breeders who have made it all possible.

Most of all, you will learn what a delight it is to own this marvelous dog. Years of enjoyment will be yours when you give your heart and home to the Bedlington Terrier.

The Bedlington

The English farmers years ago
Lost crops to otters, badgers
And other pests. I went to work
And killed or chased these cadgers.

I also did another job
That showed up all the cats.
The land was full of rodents and
I gave these rodents—rats!

I chased 'em over hill and dale
And brought 'em to their knees—
One shake and they would never swipe
Another piece of cheese.

We cut their population down
Until they ceased to matter;
In early books the Bedlington
Was classified a "ratter."

So when some Bedlingtons I know
Act too aristocratic,
My conduct, I'm afraid, is not
Exactly diplomatic.

I tell them, "Don't put on The Dog,
Go ask your mom and paters
If we're not from a humble line
Of plain exterminators."

—Woman's Home Companion

Characteristics
of the Bedlington Terrier

A common characteristic of all terriers is their desire to work with great enthusiasm and courage. They all have large and powerful teeth for the size of their bodies, and they have keen hearing and excellent eyesight. No matter how many generations they have been pets, the purpose for which the breed was bred will remain within the dog.

Darley Matheson wrote, "The Bedlington Terriers are, as a rule, first-class water dogs, keen hunters after vermin and 'game to death.'" Stonehenge wrote in 1887, "He is extremely plucky." Rine wrote in 1944, "They take to water nicely and have even proved quite capable retrievers. They are game and adaptable."

Eugene Noble wrote the following in his article on "The Gypsy Dogs:"

"He began and continued for a long while as a 'poor man's dog.' His devotees were a rough set of hardy workingmen, miners, nailers, gypsies, and tinkers, for the most part. They wanted something scrappy; a dog that would do or die; a lithe, agile, fearless gamester; the sort described by an admirer in these words, 'If he once takes a holt, heaven and yirth won't make him let go.' For running a fox or drawing a badger; for protecting a place where every friend was known and respected, and every stranger suspected and repelled; and for fighting, tenaciously and most times triumphantly, this

No matter how many generations have been bred, a terrier will retain his inherent instincts and purpose. Ch. Inverness Sybil and brother Ch. Inverness Oliver. Owned by Jim and Helen Heintz.

Bedlington Terriers make wonderful companion dogs and will happily participate in family activities. Bred by Lucy Heyman.

breed was developed. Rough men, poor men, clever and canny men, fancied and bred the Bedlington....But times change and dogs change with them. The pastimes of yesterday are sometimes the cruelties of tomorrow. Fighting, ratting, wild-animal baiting, and other pleasures of a century ago are no more, and refinement cloaks coarseness. Interest waned, breeding was curtailed, new fancies prevailed. But there were some Bedlington partisans who would not give up. They changed objectives in breeding—less fighting,

more domesticity. The little terrier became gentler, more humanized, and a pound or two heavier, and the breed found favor with new people."

The Bedlington is now a well-beloved family dog, giving much and asking little in return. He likes to have appropriate attention from the family and in return will give of himself and be a loving, contributing family member. He will be extremely loyal and is very good with children. However, in spite of his lamb-like appearance and soft looks, this is an athletic breed and every inch a terrier. This is not a breed that will while away the hours quietly in your lap, but he will be curious and enthusiastic. He loves to play and entertain, and he will be a great companion dog.

Helen Heintz wrote of the many Bedlingtons she has owned over the years, "Personally, I can laugh and cry when looking back to each and

Once you have shared your life with a Bedlington Terrier, you will find it difficult to be without one.

As the years passed, the need for the working terrier waned, and the Bedlington was bred to be a gentle, devoted, and spirited house pet.

Although he is as gentle as the lamb that he resembles, the Bedlington is an athletic dog that enjoys being outdoors. Owned by Gail Gates.

every 'love' who entered our lives. They were all different, like our offspring. I have never had a favorite Bedlington, only friends. Our breed is a winning breed in every way. Special friends, loving friends, intelligent beyond belief, and so beautiful to look at."

Once you have owned, lived with, and loved a Bedlington, you will probably find it difficult to be without one (or two or three).

Helen Heintz with Ch. Inverness Dierdre, one of the many Bedlingtons she has loved over the years.

Owning a Bedlington Terrier has always been considered to be the height of fashion. Bedlington Terrier owned by Marjorie Hanson at a 1964 fashion show.

History
of the Bedlington Terrier

⌒⁄⁄⌒

In the history of the dog world, the Bedlington Terrier is not an ancient breed, but its official beginnings, which trace back to the 1700s, place it among one of the older recognized breeds. The Bedlington Terrier belongs to the group of dogs called Terriers, from the Latin word *terra,* meaning "earth." A terrier is a dog that has been bred to work beneath the ground, driving out small and large vermin, rodents, and other animals that can be a nuisance to country living.

All of the dogs in the Terrier Group originated in the British Isles, with the exception of the Miniature Schnauzer from Germany. Many of the terrier breeds were derived from a similar ancestor, and the terriers still fall roughly into two very basic categories: the rough-coated, short-legged dogs of Scotland and the longer-legged, smooth-coated dogs of England, the group in which the Bedlington Terrier is placed.

The Bedlington Terrier hails from the mining county of Northumberland in the North of England. Originally called the Rothbury Terrier, he was bred by the miners, who loved the breed for its gameness, speed, courage, and intelligence. The Bedlington was truly a product of the working people. Darley Matheson, author of *Terriers,* wrote, "Amongst all the Terriers there is none to supersede the Bedlington so far as real game qualifications are

The Bedlington Terrier

The Bedlington Terrier's colour is blue.
His silver white top knot is splendid to view.
His eyes are small of an inky black.
The pads of his feet have never a crack.
His back is arched with a graceful sweep.
His ribs are flat and his briskit deep.
His coat is close with a curly twist.
His hocks are short with a quarter turn list.
His legs and ears have plenty of feather.
His body skin is like chamois leather.
He slopes behind, has a close straight front.
A fox or badger he'll readily hunt.
His head is long, with a sculptured dome.
Foreface filled up with solid bone.
No dish there is below those eyes.
Has a sinewy neck and muscular thighs.
A level mouth, teeth strong and white.
There is a tenacity in his bite.
He is handsome to view, glance at his jaw.
He is straight from shoulder to fore paw.
A terror when roused, though he looks so meek.
With his filbert shaped ears hung flat on his cheek.
A fight is his hobby, he cares not a jot.
A paladin in battles, he'll worry the lot.
If ought like this he's a terrier indeed.
And he never will fail you in your hour of need.

—Jack Wailes, Bedlington England

A Bedlington Terrier head study included in a pack of 30 cards appearing in the larger packets of DeReszke Cigarettes.

concerned, and anyone who has kept one of these Terriers will substantiate the truth of this statement."

The background of the breed is somewhat obscure, but it is assumed that the Old English Terrier provided the basis for the dog, with the possibility of crosses to the Otterhound and/or the Dandie Dinmont Terrier. Although the Whippet is often mentioned as a possible ancestor, there is no proof that the Whippet has any place in the pedigree. (However, it is thought that the Bedlington was, on occasion, introduced into the Whippet pedigree to give him a bit of the keenness and eagerness of the Bedlington.) It is assumed by many that the Bedlington and the Dandie are at least distant relatives. Not only did both breeds originate in the North of England, but they have the characteristics of the top-knot and the hound-like ears, unlike any other terriers.

Eugene Noble wrote in a 1936 article for the *AKC Gazette* that in the 1700s, Bedlingtons were known as "Gypsy Dogs" and were bred and used by the English Gypsies. The dogs earned the reputation of being tough and game, and they could run with a horse or hunt with a pack. They were extremely loyal, had a very keen nose, and could hold their own with almost anything. Although the men who took a liking to these dogs did not keep written records, they appreciated purposeful dogs and had an eye for breeding the best to the best. Mr. Noble wrote, "I doubt if many fanciers up in the northeast corner of England could read or write. But they could raise a dog, and rate a dog, and back a dog. These were the origins of the Rothbury Terrier, forerunner of the Bedlington."

Very early history credits a dog named "Old Flint," owned by Squire Trevelyan, as a progenitor of the breed. Although this dog was born in 1782, it is said that Bedlingtons to the mid-1800s could trace their ancestry back to "Old Flint" through a dog called "Scamp."

About 1820, Joseph Aynsley (also spelled Ainsley), of the town of Bedlington, Northumberland, purchased a dog called "Peachem," which he bred to a bitch named "Phoebe." This pair produced a liver son named "Piper" that belonged to James Anderson of Rothbury Forest. Aynsley then acquired a blue bitch by the name of "Cotes' Phoebe" (also spelled Coates), named for the vicar of the town, and this bitch was bred to "Anderson's Piper," a well-known stud dog of the time. (Note that early dogs were named after their owner. When the dog changed hands, the name would usually change to the new owners, often making it diffi-cult to trace the very old pedi-grees.) Piper must have been a true diehard, because he "lived to 15 years old, and at the age of 14, toothless and almost blind, drew a badger ... In addition, he saved Mrs. Aynsley's 14-month-old baby from an enraged sow."

An etching of the Bedlington Terrier from the Second Edition of the *Dogs of the British Isles*, published in 1872 and edited by "Stonehenge." It is one of the oldest known published pictures of the breed. *Reproduction courtesy of Basilio S. Bolumen, MD*

In 1844, a gentleman by the name of Thomas John Pickett, from Newcastle-upon-Tyne, took the Bedlington under his wing, and it was through his love of the breed that the Bedlington gained in popularity. The first dog show with a Bedlington class was held in Newcastle in 1870, with a remarkable entry of 52 competitors. *Hutchinson's Dog Encylopaedia* noted: "What a wonderful sight it must have been! 52 Bedlingtons, rugged and rough one may be sure, but none the worse for that, and every man-John of

Ch. Tyneside, owned by Thomas John Pickett, Newcastle-on-Tyne.

A rendition of Ch. Tyneside, painted by George Earl in 1869. Original oil owned by Grace Brewin.

them hard as nails, each thirsting to get his steel-trap jaws fast on his neighbor!" Mr. Pickett's dog, "Tear 'em" won first place over the large entry. In 1871, "Tyneside," also owned by Mr. Pickett, won first place in a class of 22. She was described as a beautiful blue bitch, faultless in shape, coat, and color. In 1872 at the show in Bedlington, Mr. Pickett achieved the enviable position of first place with "Tyne" (sister to "Tear 'em"). "Tear 'em" placed second, and "Tyneside" placed third.

Pickett wrote, "The Bedlington I look upon as a farmer's friend and country gentleman's companion. No breed of Terrier can compare with him for stamina, fire, courage, and resolution. He will knock about all day with his master, busy as a bee at foxes, rabbits, or otters; and at night, when any other sort of dog would be stiff, sore, and utterly jaded, he will turn up bright as a new shilling and ready for any game going. He takes to the water readily, has a capital nose, is most intelligent and lively, and as a rough and ready friend about the fields and woods, he has no equal."

Clyde Boy, an early Bedlington Terrier.

In 1877, the National Bedlington Terrier Club (of England) was formed, and by 1905 there were three Bedlington Terrier clubs in England, covering the North, South, and the Midlands. In 1906, a Bedlington won Best in Show at Ipswich, further giving the breed a firm footing in the British Isles.

Before we leave the Bedlington of the past centuries, an 1878 letter should be noted from John Stoker to a Mr. Oliver, regarding the Bedlington background: "I am now 48 years old and I can recollect perfectly when I was 10 years old what was said about the quality of the dogs then. Ned Cotes' bitch 'Phoebe' was black with white hairs and got from Jim Howe and from this the real 'stuff' was bred. He put her to the Blagdon dog and got three dog pups. Next, Joe Aynsley took her to Rothbury Forest to Jim Anderson's 'Piper.' He was a yellow dog with gray hairs and a strong dog and showed up the otter hound a little. He was said to be the gamest dog for foxes or badgers that ever had been in that part of the country. It was here where the Bedlington fanciers gained their object. They got a litter of two bitches and one dog and Joe Aynsley got the dog which we are all trying to imitate now. He was liver with wired hair and the tuft of lint on the top of his head. The old fanciers said a game and better specimen would not be found."

On a sad note, Mr. Stoker also wrote, "Ned and John Coates were leading men with their dogs, baiting the fox at the same time as their father was preaching the gospel at our village church. Ned Coates, shortly after this time, went wrong of his mind and was taken to the mad house. He begged of his friends to let 'Peachem' go with him. They consented. The dog grew that savage that no one dare go near him and he was destroyed."

THE BREED CROSSES THE ATLANTIC

The Bedlington Terrier was imported into the United States in the late 1800s, and the first entry in the American Kennel Club (AKC) Stud Book was in 1883. His popularity was not immediate in America, and Stud Book registrations remained in the very low numbers until 1924, when yearly registrations totaled ten, the highest number to that date. There were no registrations in 1884 and 1885, and one breeder registered nine dogs in 1886. Although the popularity was slow in growing in the US, the breed was becoming better known in Canada. Two litters were bred there in 1883.

AKC registrations remained low, but the Bedlington was seen at dog shows in both the US and Canada. In 1883, a specific class for Bedlingtons was given at the Chicago show. At the Toronto show in 1884, there was a large enough entry— five dogs and four bitches—that the classes were divided by sex. By this time, the breed was being entered at most of the larger US shows. In September of 1884, the first North American championship was earned by Ch. Blucher, an English dog whelped in 1882 and unregistered in the US. By 1885, a committee was formed to write a standard for the breed.

The first known American illustration of a Bedlington Terrier, from Ed James' *Terrier Dogs*, 1873, 24th Edition.

At this time, the breed was still more popular in Canada than in the States, with a Mr. Severne of Vancouver Island importing seven dogs from England between 1883 and 1888. In eastern Canada, W. S. Jackson registered nine Bedlingtons with the AKC in 1886. A friend of Mr. Jackson's from upstate New York, Mr. William Russell, registered a bitch bred by Jackson in 1887 and became the first US resident to register a Bedlington with the AKC; however, unregistered dogs had been shown in the states. Over the years, Mr. Russell remained a true American pioneer of the breed and pure-bred dogs, supporting all-breed shows, the breed club, and the AKC.

Syrup H., AKC 16,622, an early American Bedlington Terrier.

By 1900, five dogs had completed their AKC titles, about 70 Bedlingtons had been registered with the AKC, and another 100 or so were unregistered. Pet puppies sold for about $50, and show prospects could reach a price of $500, a large sum of money at the time.

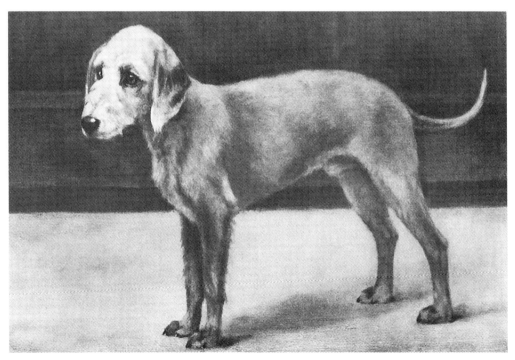

Ch. Cranley Blue Boy, bred and owned by Mr. Harold Warnes, winner of 20 Firsts, and numerous Seconds, Thirds, and Specials. He is also the winner of the 25-Guinea Cup at the Ipswich Show in 1906 for the Best Dog of the breeds entered, believed to be the first honor for a Bedlington Terrier. *Reproduction courtesy of Basilio S. Bolumen, MD*

The Guggenheims and Firenze Kennels

In 1911, as the Bedlington struggled in popularity, the breed received a tremendous boost from Col. M. Robert Guggenheim of Long Island, New York, with the importation of some top English specimens to his Firenze Kennels. The 1,100-acre Firenze Farms was described in a 1927 *AKC Gazette* article by Arthur F. Jones as follows: "It is such a place as might come to mind some night as you count the sheep jumping over the fence, for with its colonial farmhouse type of residence, its winding roads disappearing off in the distance across a miniature plainland, its many long, low farm and kennel buildings, its acres of yellow tulips, its big pasture with cows leaning over the bars, its trout stream with the rustic bridge, and finally, the Bedlingtons, those dogs with the head-profile of sheep, all bring up quiet, sleep-seducing thoughts."

Col. Guggenheim had a great interest in dogs, having at one time owned 65 Bulldogs and later adding a pack of 30 Beagles to his kennel. He was an avid hunter, and, of course, the Master of the Pack. His interest in Bedlingtons began around 1905 when he saw the breed in England and later imported some of the top English specimens. The kennel manager, Edward Ward, was from England, as almost all good kennel men were in those days. Ward traveled overseas to keep abreast of the English Bedlington scene, bringing good dogs back with him.

The Firenze Kennels were impressive. Jones wrote that there were numerous kennel buildings, including the show kennel, the puppy building, and the whelping kennel. Special trophy cabinets lined the passageways, and a small building housed the medical and cooking facilities, featuring everything that was needed for the kennel manager and other employees. There were three vehicles kept for the kennel: a station wagon, a light truck, and the touring car. Nearly 130 puppies and dogs were kept in the facility. A dozen Bedlingtons were often sent to shows at once, and the 1927 Westminster show had 26 Firenze Bedlingtons in representation. Col. Guggenheim was given much credit for the popularization of the breed, because his dogs appeared at all of the big Eastern shows. His influence was so strong during this period that of the 29 Bedlingtons that became champions between 1920 and 1930, only six were not

Christmas Carol, AKC 20,710, an early American Bedlington Terrier.

owned or co-owned by Guggenheim or Firenze Kennels. Ch. Deckham O'Lad of Firenze was the first Best in Show Bedlington, winning the all-breed show at Rochester, New York, in 1927. The role that Col. Guggenheim played in bringing the Bedlington into the eye of the public and keeping it there was an important one for the breed, even though its registered numbers in America remained small.

Between 1884, when the first Bedlington champion was listed in the AKC records, and 1920, about 80 percent of the champions were imported from the British Isles. Between 1930 and 1940, the percentages changed, and over half of the champions were now bred in the US and Canada. The Bedlingtons were fortunate to have had a very dedicated group of individuals who were responsible for this change.

The year 1931 marked the end of the Guggenheim era and the last of the Firenze champions in the record books. Also in 1931, the name McAnulty appeared for the first time. The breed was seeing a changing of the guard.

Boardwalk Kennels

Mr. and Mrs. Charles McAnulty of Boardwalk Kennels in Atlantic City, New Jersey, acquired Garw Warrior of Leeds in 1928. Two champions of record were produced when this dog was bred to the blue British import, Caroline, and another champion was produced when he was bred to Boardwalk Nuts. Up to that time, this was the first stud dog to produce three American champions. The English dog Moving Night was one of four Bedlingtons that Col. Guggenheim imported to the US. Elizabeth Cooper wrote: "Moving Night is of importance because all Bedlingtons, however they have been bred, are bred down from him again and again and again. This had a stabilizing effect upon the breed." Widely used in England, Moving Night sired more Bedlington champions than any other dog up to that time.

Anthony and Anna Neary

In 1929, Anthony Neary and his wife Anna of Bedlington, England, arrived in the US with a pair of Bedlingtons. They rented a small house on Long Island and proceeded to breed these dogs with the hope of introducing their favorite breed to America. They put their very limited funds into breeding and attending Eastern dog shows on the weekends, driving up to the show sites in their ramshackle car, competing with the wealthy owners' dogs and their handlers. Anna Neary wrote that at the 1930 Westminster show, these two very green but enthusiastic Bedlington owners met Dr. McAnulty, and the three of them spent the following three afternoons sitting on the benches together discussing the breed. Thus, a lifelong friendship formed.

The Nearys and the Rockefellers

The two dogs that the Nearys brought from England were registered in America as Exiled Laddie and Hasty Morn. In 1932, Exiled Laddie became an American champion and eventually sired six champions. At the 1940 Westminster show, a Neary dog was selected Best American-Bred Terrier. Later, the Nearys received a call from Mr. William Rockefeller, who had seen the dog at Westminster. Within a year, Mr. Rockefeller purchased the Neary's dog and retained Anthony as kennel manager. The team of the Rockefellers and the Nearys were a major influence and a force to be reckoned with, not only in the Bedlington ring but in the Terrier Group up until the time that the Nearys retired in 1965. The Nearys also did some breeding of their own under the Tyneside prefix.

Ch. Exiled Laddie, owned by Anthony and Anna Neary. An English import, he became an American champion and sired six champions.

The Nearys devoted their lives to the Bedlington Terrier and to the improvement of the breed. The Rockefellers, with their great wealth, were able to support the Nearys in their quest for the continual improvement of the Bedlington. Through the coupling of talents and money on a scale of this type, the rare breed of the Bedlington Terrier was ensured survival and popularity on American shores. In addition, both families were strong supporters of the Bedlington Terrier Club of America (BTCA), with Mrs. Neary as one of the founding members and Mr. Rockefeller serving as president.

OTHER NOTABLE FANCIERS

Other fanciers from the 1930s should be mentioned before we come back to the Rockefellers. Although these fanciers' active periods were shorter-lived than the Rockfeller dynasty, each one had an impact on the breed.

Sanford Freund of Ashtoncroft Kennels in Ridgefield, Connecticut, had three champions sired by the Nearys' Ch. Exiled Laddie, and all three were out of Freund's Duchess of Ashtoncroft. All told, Mr. Freund owned 12 champions. In 1936, he donated a trophy to the BTCA for the Bred-by-Exhibitor classes to encourage the breeding of the Bedlington. He was an active breeder and exhibitor from 1935 to 1941 and also served as president of the national club.

Dr. Eugene Noble was another fancier active from about 1935 to 1943. Dr. Noble finished numerous dogs, of which two were Welsh imports and four were English imports. He was also a writer,

A boy and his Bedlingtons, from *Hutchinson's Dog Encyclopedia*, 1935.

contributing to the breed archives an article that was published in the June 1936 *AKC Gazette* on the "Gypsy Dogs."

Mr. and Mrs. John Breedon of Sarasota, California, were active in the breed in the middle and late 1930s under the Springdale prefix, finishing four champions. They were also very active in the formation of the Bedlington Terrier Club of the West.

Ch. Kirkhill Exquisite, an English import that was a multiple group winner both in America and England. Owned by Gertrude Boeckman.

Gertrude Boeckman, of St. Paul, Minnesota, was also breeding and showing her dogs during this period, finishing four champions, one of which was co-owned by the Nearys and sired by Ch. Exiled Laddie. She also owned Ch. Kirkhill Exquisite, an English import that was a multiple group winner both on her home turf and at the Eastern shows. Judge Alfred Lupine said that she was one of the best of all time, a beauty and a sensation. Dr. Eugene Noble owned one of her sons. The *AKC Blue Book of Dogs* notes that "Miss Boeckman raised 13 pups under temperature conditions in Minnesota which varied from 100 degrees above zero to 30 below zero without a single fatality. And that is something."

Rowanoaks Kennels

In 1936, Col. and Mrs. P. V. G. Mitchell of Summit, New Jersey (Rowanoaks Kennels), acquired a Bedlington puppy as a housepet. With the encouragement of the breeder, their daughter, Connie Willemsen, started showing the dog, who within six months became Ch. Baron Conrad. The Mitchells realized that although their dog performed well, he lacked certain qualities that they were looking for in the breed. In 1939, they traveled to England to visit the Bedlington kennels and brought back to the US two outstanding specimens, now known in the record books as the dog, Ch. Tarragona of Rowanoaks and the bitch, Ch. Love Letter. Tarragona was immediately a top-winning Bedlington and remained so until a year later, when his daughter, Ch. Lady Rowena of Rowanoaks, exceeded him. Lady Rowena had a sparkle about her that caught the judges' eye when she walked into the ring. In 1938, she was Best in Show at the Rhode Island Kennel Club while still in the puppy class. In 1939, she was Best in Show at the Westbury Kennel Club and, the same year, Best in Show at the prestigious

Montgomery County All-Terrier Show. In addition, she had 12 Group Firsts and numerous group placements, all accomplished under three different owners. Ch. Love Letter, the bitch imported with Tarragona, also did well in the ring, with a Group Third at Morris and Essex in 1938 and a Group Fourth in 1937 at the Ladies Dog Club show.

Ch. Lady Rowena of Rowanoaks, a top-winning Bedlington in the late 1930s. Owned by Rowanoaks Kennels.

The Rowanoaks advertisement read, "First, we breed for temperament, then type and soundness. We also stress beautiful heads, profuse coats, and good bone." The Mitchells were well-known as breeders who looked for and bred correct type. They kept no more than 12 dogs, and each dog in training for the show ring received two miles of road work every day. Nearly 100 champions have come out of the Rowanoaks kennels, and hundreds more have the Rowanoaks name in their backgrounds. In the late 1960s, Bob Wendell of Tartania Kennels became the Rowanoaks handler and finished many more notable dogs and bitches for the Mitchells.

Connie Willemsen with her father, Col. P. V. G. Mitchell, founder of Rowanoaks Kennels, in the early 1940s.

Connie Willemsen with her son Alan Willemsen in 1941.

Connie Willemsen currently lives in Scottsdale, Arizona, and is a past president of the BTCA. Her son Alan is also a member of the club, making them possibly the only three-generation family of Bedlington owners. Mrs. Willemsen is an AKC-licensed judge and has nearly 50 years in experience of breeding and exhibiting Bedlingtons.

Canis

E. M. J. Funkhouser was another very active breeder in the middle 1940s through the 1950s. Her first Bedlington was Theodora the Iplet, out of excellent English stock. The dam of this bitch was owned by the head of the zoology department at Swarthmore College, where Miss Funkhouser was majoring in zoology. She attended her first dog show in 1939, the Morris and Essex show, and watched Ch. Tarragona of Rowanoaks go Best of Opposite Sex against his daughter, Ch. Lady Rowena of Rowanoaks, handled by Anthony Neary. When she decided to breed "Teddy," she chose to go to Rowanoaks Kennel and their star, Tarragona. With this first litter, the kennel name of Canis appeared, inspired by the scientist in Miss Funkhouser. Canis Prima, Canis Secundus, Canis Tertia, Canis Quartus, and Canis Quinta were all products of this first litter. She later bred Canis Quartus and Canis Quinta and produced a litter of 12 puppies around the time that Pearl Harbor was bombed in 1941. That must still be a near-record-size Bedlington litter.

When World War II broke out, Rowanoaks Kennels temporarily disbanded (as many kennels did during that era), and Miss

Funkhouser took in several of the dogs, including Tarragona, who lived out his life with her. She said that he was the smartest, most intelligent and rewarding pet that she had ever had. He passed his marvelous spirit on to those he produced—proud, alert, head up, and ready for any action—the true terrier spirit.

Miss Funkhouser wrote a charming article about her life with Bedlingtons that appeared in the winter 1974 *BTCA Bulletin.* Writing as a true breeder, she mentions her successes and the planning behind her breeding. She also writes, "Of course, out of 53 litters (205 registered puppies) there were many that were more or less failures. And many that were successful, but not important enough to mention particularly." If only all breeders would be so honest about their stock!

Ch. Canis Laris, a top-winning show dog and sire of Ch. Rock Ridge Night Rocket. Owned by Mr. and Mrs. L. H. Terpening.

Eng. Am. Can. Ch. Foggyfurze Classic Cut, bred by Fred Gent, was a well-known sire for Mr. and Mrs. L. H. Terpening.

Mr. and Mrs. L. H. Terpening

Mr. and Mrs. L. H. Terpening of Princeton, New Jersey, bred and showed their dogs in the 1940s. They purchased Canis Laris from E. M. J. Funkhouser in 1943. Laris was not only an all-breed Best-in-Show dog, but made his mark in the breed as the sire of the Rockefellers' Ch. Rock Ridge Night Rocket. Another well-known sire from this kennel was the English import, Eng. Am. Ch. Foggyfurze Classic Cut, bred by Fred Gent, whelped in 1952, and handled by Percy Roberts (who went on to become a highly regarded all-breed judge). Ch. Janice Blue Tango, sired by Foggyfurze, became a top-producing dam, with seven champion offspring.

Mr. Terpening served on the BTCA board of directors at various times in the capacities of bulletin editor, secretary, and president. The Terpenings were active in the breed as late as the early 1980s, with Mr. Terpening still serving on the BTCA board at that time.

The Rockefellers and Rock Ridge Kennels

The Rockefellers, under the kennel name of Rock Ridge, and with the assistance of the Nearys, were truly a dominant force in the breed. Champions continued to come out of the kennel into the early 1960s. The outstanding dog, still considered to be a pillar of the breed, was Ch. Rock Ridge Night Rocket, whelped in 1946. His sire, Ch. Canis Laris, was a Best in Show winner, and his dam, Ch. Rock Ridge Rockette, was out of Ch. Neary's Leedsagain, dam of six champions.

Night Rocket's show career was unexcelled by almost any dog of any breed. He may not have scored the quantity of Bests in Show that some current dogs achieve, but the quality and prestige of the shows that he won was exceptional. At a little over one year of age, he was Best in Show from the Open Dog Class at the famous and prestigious Morris and Essex show. This show was held at Giralda Farms, the private estate of Geraldine Dodge. The following February, he was Best in Show at Westminster, and the following year he repeated his Morris and Essex win, retiring the Best in Show trophy from that show. Judge Alva Rosenberg, now deceased but considered one of the top dog men of all time, said, "Without reservation, Night Rocket is one of the best I've seen in 38 years of judging." John Rendall of the *New York Times* wrote: "The popularity of the victory was evident from the roar that went up from a large remnant of a crowd of 15,000 when Rosenberg sent Night Rocket to the center stage." He was shown only 23 times with 9 Group Firsts and placed in the group all but one time. He was used sparingly at stud, but in a short and limited career he

Ch. Rock Ridge Night Rocket, winning Best in Show at Westminster Kennel Club, February 12, 1948.

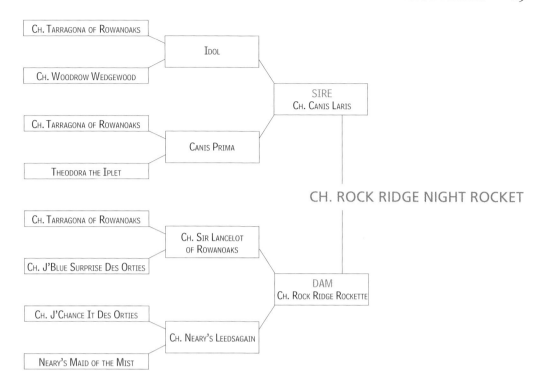

CH. TARRAGONA OF ROWANOAKS		
	IDOL	
CH. WOODROW WEDGEWOOD		
		SIRE
		CH. CANIS LARIS
CH. TARRAGONA OF ROWANOAKS		
	CANIS PRIMA	
THEODORA THE IPLET		

CH. ROCK RIDGE NIGHT ROCKET

CH. TARRAGONA OF ROWANOAKS		
	CH. SIR LANCELOT OF ROWANOAKS	
CH. J'BLUE SURPRISE DES ORTIES		
		DAM
		CH. ROCK RIDGE ROCKETTE
CH. J'CHANCE IT DES ORTIES		
	CH. NEARY'S LEEDSAGAIN	
NEARY'S MAID OF THE MIST		

Breeder: Mr. & Mrs. William Rockefeller
Owner: Mr. & Mrs. William Rockefeller

sired 36 champions. Gordon Cunningham wrote in *Terrier Type,* "The greatest judges have considered him one of the soundest and overall excellent dogs of all time...many waves have hit the sand but few as high as Ch. Rock Ridge Night Rocket. When studying the many lovely photos of him I hear the barks of puppies, now several generations removed from this all-time great, but a very definite reminder that here was a great dog, never to be forgotten." Night Rocket was always handled by Anthony Neary. The *AKC Gazette* wrote, "For the Nearys, at long last, was acknowledgment of their favorite breed and that their unending effort had not been in vain." The *BTCA Bulletin* of 1957 noted, "Were there more people like the William A. Rockefellers how much nicer it would be. The Bedlington is indeed fortunate in having the Rockefellers behind them."

Bo-Peep Kennels
Wilda Woehr of Bo-Peep Kennels in Columbia City, Indiana, was an active breeder in the 1940s and 1950s and was both a handler and an AKC-licensed judge. She was an active Bedlington fancier up until the time of her death. It would be hard to outdo Miss Woehr's description of her beginnings with Bedlingtons, which

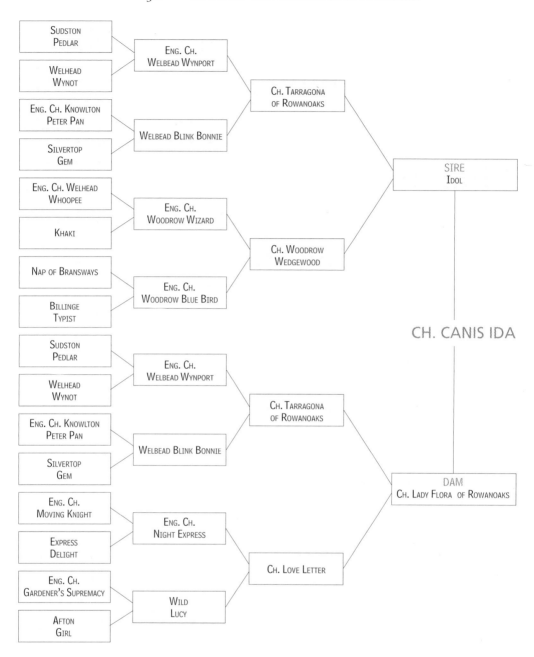

Breeder: Elizabeth Funkhouser
Owner: Dorothy E. Morrison

appeared in an article in the spring 1974 *BTCA Bulletin*. "When I purchased my first one I had never even seen a picture of one. I really didn't know what to expect except that the written descriptions were exactly what I wanted in a dog. In a very heavy snowstorm I met three trains from the East and not one had a little dog for me, but I was assured she would be on the next train at 3 am. My father and I got up in the night and met the train and there she was! I became a member of the local kennel club and heard there was a Bedlington entered at the Detroit show and Mother and I made the trip in excited anticipation. That year I made my first trip to Morris and Essex to see the Bedlingtons entered there and from then on, it was two trips East a year. I saw many great dogs at the Specialty and Westminster shows in February and the Morris and Essex show in May. Early in my experience I saw Ch. Rowena of Rowanoaks do her thing in the ring...she has always represented the specimen nearest the standard to me to this day. She was a true showman, always on her toes, selling herself to the judge and the ringside."

As the 1950s neared, the dog world had seen two great Bedlington Terrier sires: Ch. Tarragona of Rowanoaks in the 1930s, sire of 23 champions; and Ch. Rock Ridge Night Rocket, who not only had a fabulous show career but was the sire of 36 champions. The bitches included Ch. Neary's Leedsagain, dam of 7 champions in the 1930s; and in the 1940s, Ch. Bo-Peep's Blue Antonia, dam of 12 champions, and Ch. Canis Ida, dam of 7 champions.

THE 1950s AND 1960s

The decades of the 1950s and 1960s saw a tremendous change in the Bedlington breed. In 1948, 218 Bedlingtons were registered, and in 1958, registrations had jumped to 573. Within another 10 years, in 1968, registrations were up to 778.

New breeders with winning dogs were coming on board during the late 1940s and 1950s, while many of the old guard continued to breed fine specimens. As in the past, the stalwarts of the breed were the Rockefellers (Rock Ridge), the Terpenings (Hollister), Wilda Woehr (Bo-Peep), E. M. J. Funkhouser (Canis), and Connie Willemsen (Rowanoaks).

Braemar Kennels

In 1946, Dorothy Morrison, Braemar Kennels, Chatham, New Jersey, first appeared in the AKC records with Ch. Canis Floris and Ch. Canis Ida, litter brother and sister, sired by Idol, out of Ch. Canis Prima. Ch. Canis Ida, a double Ch. Tarragona of Rowanoaks granddaughter, went on to become a top producer, dam of seven champions. Mrs. Morrison was active into the 1970s, breeding many more champions.

Ch. Idol, sire of Ch. Canis Ida.

Hughcliff Kennels

Eunice and Evelyn Clark, Hughcliff Kennels, Hinckley, Ohio, bred Ch. Hughcliff Hughie in 1947, sired by Ch. Rock Ridge Night Rocket, out of Ch. Rock Ridge Emblem. In 1948, "Hughie" and two of his litter sisters finished their championships. Hughie produced several champions but made his mark in the breed

CH. HUGHCLIFF BLUE TYLER

Breeder: Eunice and Evelyn Clark
Owner: E. Wasserman and E. Wasserman

through one of his progeny, Ch. Hughcliff Blue Tyson, whelped in 1956. "Tyson" became a top producer with 17 champion get, of which one was Ch. Hughcliff Blue Tyler, whelped in 1959. "Tyler," following in the footsteps of his father, also became a top producer, equaling his sire's record with 17 champion get. The Hughcliff Kennels name appears throughout the 1950s. Eunice Clark also served as secretary of the BTCA.

Cascadental Kennels

Mr. and Mrs. Carl Roth from Bardonia, New York (Cascadental Kennels), contributed to the Bedlington in several areas. They finished many champions during the 1950s and 1960s, with

Cascadental Nemesis, CD, as the outstanding dog of their kennel. Whelped in 1960, she went on to become a top producer with eight champion get. As busy as she may have been in the whelping box, she found time to add an obedience degree to her name. In addition to breeding, Mr. Roth became a jewelry maker, turning out marvelous Bedlington jewelry and sculpture pieces. He made more than 200 Bedlington jewelry items in gold, silver, bronze, and other metals. Those who have one of his pieces

An example of Bedlington sculpture by Mr. Carl Roth of Cascadental Kennels.

indeed has a treasure, as he produced works of great quality depicting Bedlingtons in a large variety of stances and head studies. Bedlington fanciers have yet to see another artist produce such fine works of art to celebrate the breed.

Tiffany Hall

Elisabeth Gray Brewer of Ovid, New York, served on the BTCA's board in the 1950s and was vice president of the national club in the 1960s. Under the Tiffany Hall prefix, she and Elisabeth David had a small breeding program that influenced the new look of the 1960s—long necks, long clean heads, and splendid hindquarters. The progeny of their Eng. Can. Am. Ch. Mirage of Wynbriar and Ch. Miss Tor of Rowanoaks ("Mirage") all left their mark on the breed, and their names can be found in the pedigrees of today's dogs. Mirage was Best of Breed twice at the Morris and Essex shows. Ch. Gemar's Lord Jeffrey, sire of 35 champions, was a grandson of this breeding.

Marvay Kennels

Martha McVay of Marvay Kennels has been active in the breed for 45 years. Her first champions, finished in the mid-1950s, were Ch. McLean's Little Colonel and Ch. Missey Valgo of Silver Crest.

Out of their first litter, five champions were produced, in addition to Ch. Marvay's Knight Errant finishing his CD and CDX. In 1964, Ch. Brandy Hi's Toddy of Marvay and, in 1966, SuBeau's Most Precious Marvay were in the top ten. Their offspring had specialty wins in 1971, '72, '78, '82, '83, and '87, in addition to an all-breed Best in Show. There were a good number of group wins and placements, plus a breed win at the Westminster Kennel Club show. Martha has been a very active and dedicated member of the

Ch. McLean's Little Colonel, one of Martha McVay's first Bedlington champions.

BTCA, serving as a board member and president, in addition to being an active member of the BTC of the West for many years. Martha revised, illustrated, and edited the "Grooming and Trimming" booklet for the BTCA and was a great help in the preparation of this book.

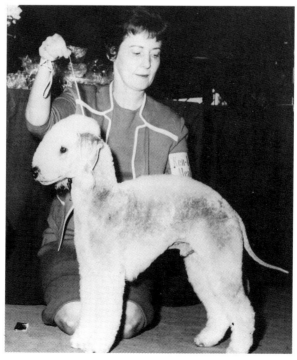

Ch. Brandy's Hi's Toddy of Marvay with owner Martha McVay.

Ch. Marvay's Penny Ante winning Best of Breed at Westminster Kennel Club in 1971. Owned by Martha McVay.

Ch. SuBeau's Most Precious Marvay winning First in Group, 1968. Owned by Martha McVay.

Ch. Marvay's Matilda Jane winning all-breed Best in Show. Owned by Martha McVay.

Ch. Marvay's Amanda Sue, a multiple Specialty winner, winning Second in Group in 1976. Owned by Martha McVay.

Ch. Marvay's Tyson, shown here in 1978 finishing her championship at one year of age. Owned by Martha McVay.

Ch. Siwash Iliza Doolittle winning First in Group in 1982. Owned by Martha McVay.

Ch. Marvay's Lady Capulet winning Veteran Class in 1985. Owned by Martha McVay.

Ch. Marvay's Minerva, a top-producing bitch with 10 champion offspring, winning Best in Sweepstakes at the Great Lakes Terrier Association in 1985. Owned by Martha McVay.

Ch. Maeb's Bobbybleu finished his championship in six shows, winning Best of Breed at five of them. Owned, bred, and handled by Martha McVay.

Valgo Kennels

Milo and Marjorie Hanson of Coronado, California, and their Valgo Kennels became well-known throughout the 1950s and 1960s. Marge had her first Bedlington in 1940, seven years before she married Milo. Not only have they bred over 75 champions, but Milo found the breed easy to train and put companion degrees in obedience on several Bedlingtons. At one show, they had three dogs entered in obedience, and all three scored 190 or better out of 200 points. Ch. Actor's Agent O'Neta, a Night Rocket daughter bred to Ch. Hamblin's Tim Beau, a Night Rocket son, produced their first home-bred champions in 1951. This was "Neta's" only litter, producing Ch. Night Editor of Valgo, Ch. Night of Valgo CD, Ch. Starlight of Valgo, and Ch. Twilight of Valgo. Most of their champions trace back to these four dogs. Marge's favorites were Ch. Valgo's Whirlwind and Ch. Gould's Top Flight of Valgo (sired by Ch. Power's Adventurer). Whirlwind was a bitch of correct size, undefeated in

Ch. Night Express of Valgo, bred and owned by Milo and Marjorie Hanson, shown here with judge Glenn Fancy and handler Milo Hanson.

Ch. Van-da's Snowcap of Valgo, an excellent example from the Valgo Kennels. Owned by Marjorie Hanson.

Ch. Flying High of Valgo, with breeder/owner/handler Marjorie Hanson.

the classes, and a top producer with seven champion get. Her son, Top Flight, owned and handled by Jack Gould, was the top-winning Bedlington of 1967. He was also a top producer with 21 champion get. Milo passed away in 1996, and Marge continues to be active in judging the Terrier Group and in the BTCA and BTC of the West and has served on the board of both clubs for many years. Marge noted: "My Bedlingtons have also helped raise two children, as well as two grandchildren. All of the children have participated in and enjoyed showing this wonderful breed."

Ralph Hogancamp with his first Bedlington, Valgo's Scampi, and judge Milo Hanson.

Ch. Valgo's Scampi with owner/handler Ralph Hogancamp and the renowned judge Alva Rosenberg.

Janice Kennels

Marie D'Andrea of Janice Kennels in New Mexico had a top-producing bitch, Ch. Janice Blue Tango, whelped in 1955 and dam of seven champions. She was a Foggyfurze Classic Cut daughter, linebred on her dam's side to Night Rocket. Mr. and Mrs. D'Andrea bred for many years, and the Janice name appears in the back of many pedigrees.

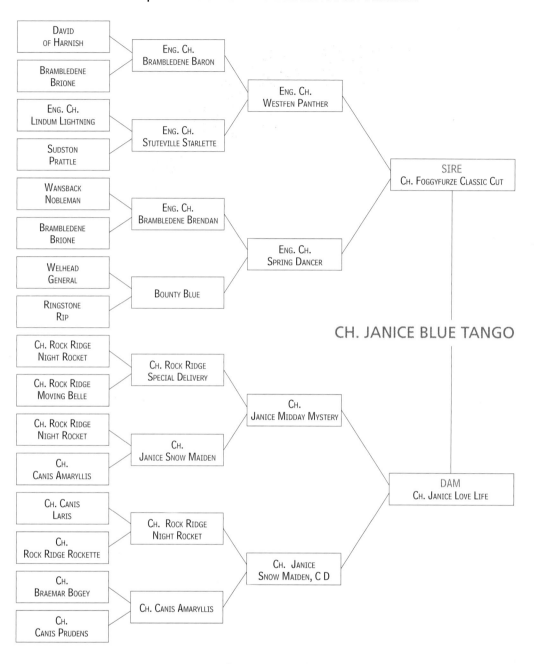

DAVID OF HARNISH			
BRAMBLEDENE BRIONE	ENG. CH. BRAMBLEDENE BARON		
ENG. CH. LINDUM LIGHTNING		ENG. CH. WESTFEN PANTHER	
SUDSTON PRATTLE	ENG. CH. STUTEVILLE STARLETTE		SIRE CH. FOGGYFURZE CLASSIC CUT
WANSBACK NOBLEMAN			
BRAMBLEDENE BRIONE	ENG. CH. BRAMBLEDENE BRENDAN		
WELHEAD GENERAL		ENG. CH. SPRING DANCER	
RINGSTONE RIP	BOUNTY BLUE		

CH. JANICE BLUE TANGO

CH. ROCK RIDGE NIGHT ROCKET			
CH. ROCK RIDGE MOVING BELLE	CH. ROCK RIDGE SPECIAL DELIVERY		
CH. ROCK RIDGE NIGHT ROCKET		CH. JANICE MIDDAY MYSTERY	
CH. CANIS AMARYLLIS	CH. JANICE SNOW MAIDEN		DAM CH. JANICE LOVE LIFE
CH. CANIS LARIS			
CH. ROCK RIDGE ROCKETTE	CH. ROCK RIDGE NIGHT ROCKET		
CH. BRAEMAR BOGEY		CH. JANICE SNOW MAIDEN, C D	
CH. CANIS PRUDENS	CH. CANIS AMARYLLIS		

Breeder: Marie D'Andrea
Owner: Marie D'Andrea and M. J. Lachapelle

Fred and Margaret Young

Fred and Margaret Young of Burbank, California, bought their first dog from Valgo Kennels. Their big winners, co-owned with Bee Spencer, were Ch. Fremar's Cable Car and Ch. Fremar's Cable Dancer. Cable Car had 4 all-breed Bests in Show, 29 Group Firsts and 4 specialty Bests in Show. In between his days on the show circuit, he sired 12 champion offspring. Cable Dancer had three all-breed Bests in Show, seven Group Firsts, and one specialty Best in Show. Mr. Young passed away in 1987, and Mrs. Young-Renihan continues to be a popular judge throughout the country.

Ch. Fremar's Cable Car retired with over 120 Bests of Breed, numerous Group Firsts, 4 Bests in Show, and was the winner of 6 Bedlington Terrier Club of the West Specialties. Owned by Fred and Margaret Young and Bee Spencer.

Lucy Jane Myers

Lucy Jane Myers of Duluth, Minnesota, although not a Bedlington breeder per se, was well-known in the dog world with her Irish Setters. She bred Ch. Draherin Blue Andante (Ch. Rock Ridge Night Rocket ex Ch. Janice Blue Tango), who was purchased by the Rockefellers and shown by Anthony Neary. In 1958, he had two all-breed Bests in Show, five Group Firsts, and placed eighth in the Terrier Group.

Center Ridge

Robert and Paula Scherff, Milwaukee, Wisconsin, purchased their first Bedlington from Charlie Prager, a popular handler, in 1954. In December of that year, they won their first Best of Breed with Ch. Snowball of Valgo, purchased from Marge Hanson. They chose the name Center Ridge for the kennel, and with Mr. Prager handling their dogs, Center Ridge quickly became a well-known name in the ring. The kennel finished approximately 30 champions, and the following "stars" emerged. Ch. Center Ridge Snow Classic, whelped in 1955 (Ch. Foggyfurze Classic Cut ex Ch. Van Dee's Snowdust of Valgo) was the winner of 5 Bests in Show, 40 Group Firsts and produced 4 champion get. She was fifth in the Terrier Group in 1956 and third in the Group in 1957. Am. and Can. Ch. Center Ridge Minute Man, whelped in 1958 and sired by Ch. Canis Furor, had two Bests in Show, was eighth in the Terrier Group in 1962, and sired nine champion get. Am. and Can. Ch. Center Ridge Lady Caroline, whelped in 1959, had a total of 15 Bests in Show, 62 Group Firsts, and 2 champion get. She was fourth in the Terrier Group in 1960 and 1961. Mr. and Mrs. Scherff were honorary life members

Breeder/judge Acquina Meyer awarding Reserve Winners to Ch. Inverness Patience at Westminster Kennel Club in 1978 with owner/handler Jim Heintz.

of the BTC of Greater Chicago. When Mr. Prager retired as kennel manager and handler for the Scherffs, Center Ridge terminated its breeding and exhibiting program.

Barbeedon Kennels

Dr. and Mrs. D. L. Cassidy, Barbeedon Kennels, Monticello, Iowa, finished Ch. Comet's Ace of Barbeedon in 1959 (Ch. Canis Furor ex Ch. Center Ridge Comet). Handled by Charlie Prager, he was 6th in the Terrier Group in 1959 with 3 Bests in Show, received 22 Group Firsts, and was the sire of 5 champion get.

Alquina

Acquina Meyer finished her first champion with the Alquina prefix in 1958, out of a bitch that her husband bought her in 1954. Mrs. Meyer was an active breeder for many years and has served on the BTCA board in various capacities, including three years as president. Ch. Alquina's Diamond was a multiple-group-winning and Best-in-Show dog, handled by Tom Gannon. Mrs. Meyer has been a judge of many terrier breeds, as well as Poodles.

Gene and Mary McGuire

In the 1960s, Gene and Mary McGuire purchased Glen Acres Gay Fancy, who was their foundation bitch. Fancy produced

Ch. Alquina's Sportsman, winning Best of Breed at Westminster Kennel Club in 1963. Owned by Gene and Mary McGuire.

Ch. Gemar's Lord Jeffrey, a top producer and multiple Best in Show winner, winning Best of Winners at the 1964 BTCA New York Specialty. Owned by Gene McGuire and handled by Edgar Duckett.

Brother and sister Ch. Gemar's Lord Jeffrey and Ch. Gemar's Merri Kim. Bred and owned by Gene McGuire.

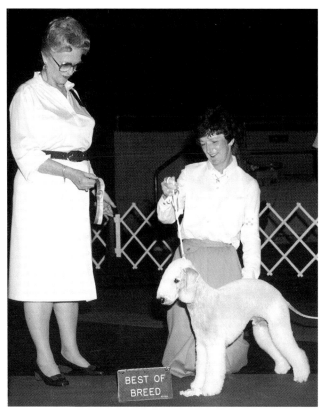

Ch. Gemar's Marksman of Sanistar. Bred, owned, and handled by Gene McGuire.

Gene McGuire, handling her own Bedlingtons to a Best in Show Brace win at the Chicago International Kennel Club in 1973.

Ch. Jolee Jingle Bells of Dovern with well-known handler Joe Waterman. Owned by Dorothy and Vern Gangwish.

five champions in two litters. The McGuires then acquired Alquina's Sportsman, who quickly became a champion and was specialed with many Bests of Breed and group placements. Gene wrote, "He was a wonderfully personable dog with beautiful conformation, and he was a joy to have every day of his life." Sportsman sired Ch. Gemar's Lord Jeffrey, another pillar of the breed, who was a top producer for several years in a row, with more than 35 champion offspring. In addition, he was a multiple all-breed Best in Show winner and the winner of six National Specialties. He was a happy dog with a wonderful personality. In addition to his show and siring career, he was a great "Show and Tell" dog for the grandchildren. Gene wrote, "We will never waver from the high standard we set in the 1960s, and we will continue to be honest in our breeding program with typey, healthy, happy, winning puppies." Gene's support and assistance with information and pictures was extremely helpful in the writing of this book.

Dorothy and Vern Gangwish

Ch. Gemar's Lord Jeffrey was the sire of Ch. Jolee Jingle Bells of Dovern, whelped in 1966. Jingles was owned by Dorothy and Vern

Gangwish. The Gangwishes were Italian Greyhound breeders in Casper, Wyoming, land of very few Bedlingtons. Vern learned his grooming from pictures, and the well-known California handler, Joe Waterman, used to comment on the "strangely trimmed" Bedlington that he saw at the shows. The two men became friends, and Joe took over the handling and grooming of Jingles. Jingles was the winner of 9 all-breed Bests in Show, 67 Group Firsts, and 7 specialty Bests in Show. He was the sire of 36 champions, of which 4 were top producers.

From right to left, Am. Can. Ch. Chimneyhouse Firecracker, CD, owned by Lois J. D'Ambrosio, with his grandsons Ch. Hall of Fame and Ch. Prize Cup Cake.

Chimneyhouse

Lois J. D'Ambrosio established the Chimneyhouse prefix in 1963. Her small breeding program has produced 12 American champions and 14 Canadian champions, in addition to many obedience-titled Bedlingtons. Am. Can. Ch. Chimneyhouse Loving Spoonful and Am.

From left to right, owner/handler Claire Poirier with Ch. Cap MaGitane Bien Aimee, owner/handler/breeder Lois D'Ambrosio with Ch. Chimneyhouse Loving Spoonful, and owner/handler Idella Cameron with Ch. Chimneyhouse Lionhearted Jed.

Can. Ch. Chimneyhouse Firecracker Am. Can. DC both had multiple group placements in the past. Am. Can. Ch. Chimneyhouse Bobby Dazzler, owned by Vicki Petris, is also a winner of multiple group placements.

Southwind Kennels

Mrs. Marion Cabage from Indiana, of Southwind Kennels, was active throughout the 1960s, and her kennel name first appeared in the record books in 1959 with Ch. South Wind's Sno-Fluff of Valgo. Her most famous dog was Ch. South Wind's Blue Velvet (Ch. South Wind's Don Juan ex Ch. South Wind's Sno-Fluff of Valgo) shown to his championship by Marian and shown through the remainder of his show career by Jack Funk. He was the top Bedlington in 1968 and the top terrier in 1969, the year that he was the recipient of the Kennel Review award. He had a total of 18 Bests in Show and 125 Group Wins, and he completed his Bermuda championship by winning two groups. He was the top Bedlington sire in 1970, 1971, 1973, and 1975, and sired a total of 32 champions.

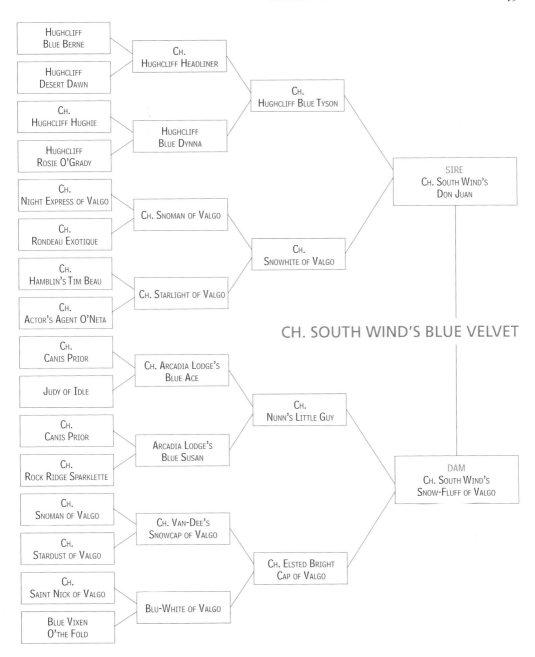

CH. SOUTH WIND'S BLUE VELVET

Breeder: Marion Cabage
Owner: Marion Cabage

Ch. South Wind's Blue Velvet, top Bedlington Terrier in 1968 and top Terrier in 1969. He had a total of 18 Bests in show and 125 Group wins, and sired a total of 32 champions. Owned by Marion Cabage.

Tartania Kennels

Delores and Bob Wendell, a well-known couple in the breed, got their foundation stock from the Clarks' Hughcliff Kennels. Their Tartania Kennels in Ohio were well known. Bob eventually became the handler for Connie Willemsen at Rowanoaks Kennels. The Wendells' Ch. Hughcliff Blue Tania was a group winner and a top producer in the mid-1960s.

Ch. Power's Adventurer, a multiple group winner and sire of 25 champion offspring. Owned by Mr. and Mrs. Robert Elder.

Mr. and Mrs. Robert Elder

Mr. and Mrs. Robert Elder of California bred and finished many champions throughout the 1960s. Their Ch. Power's Adventurer was a multiple group winner, with 80 Bests of Breed to his name. Whelped in 1958, the key dog in his pedigree was Ch. Rock Ridge Night Rocket. He went down as a top producer with 25 champion get, the most notable being Ch. Gould's Top Flight of Valgo, owned by Jack Gould, who was also a group winner and a top producer, sire of 21 champions.

CH. POWER'S ADVENTURER

Breeder: Claire A. Hannigan and Marie D'Andrea
Owner: Robert W. and Patricia Elder

Petercrest Kennel

Another kennel that was popular in the 1960s was Grace Brewin's Petercrest Kennel. Not only did she breed many champions, but she was also an active member of the BTCA, serving as president. She was the owner of Ch. Barbeedon's Merry Morn, dam of four champions. She is also an AKC judge of the Terrier Group, the Sporting Group, and several hound breeds.

Ch. Titica's Gay Cinnamon Cindy, Number One Terrier Bitch in 1973. Owned by Allan Sheimo and Basilio S. Bolumen.

NOTABLE DOGS

Among other notable dogs and breeders was Ch. Titaca's Gay Cinnamon Cindy, Number One Terrier Bitch in 1973 and the first liver bitch to win an all-breed Best in Show. She was owned by Allan Sheimo and Basilio Bolumen of Chicago. Another of their dogs, Ch. Teaka's Sonny Too V Chrisandra, handled by Bobby Hutton, finished his cham pionship with four majors and four group placements. Ch. Elder's Bourbon, whelped in 1967, bred by Robert Elder and owned by Roger Widener and Jack Denst, was the dam of

Ch. Chrisandra's Foxfire Vixen with Chuck Pastorius, Ch. Teaka's Sonny Too V Chrisandra with Bob Hutton, Ch. Chrisandra's Fiesty Fox with Steve Cochrane, Ch. Chrisandra's Foxy Leide with Marion Cabage and Ch. Chrisandra's Frostfire Vixen with Allen Sheimo. Brood bitch class, BTCA New York Specialty, 1974.

10 champions. Roger also bred and owned Ch. Bourbon's Apollo of Victoria, a Best in Show dog sired by Ch. Lucinda's Tim of Gold Grove. Sally DeKold's Am. Can. Ch. Sunburst of Tamarack was all-breed Best in Show in 1971. Ch. Shelbyshire's Blaze to Glory, owner-handled by Mr. and Mrs. Michael Padula of Florida, was an all-breed Best in Show winner, the top Bedlington in 1967, and one of the top terriers of the year.

Some wonderful dogs, show specimens, and top-producing sires and dams were whelped during these years, and they had a lasting impact on the breed. Nearly every pedigree, carried back far enough, will have the following names:

- Ch. Tarragona of Rowanoaks, an English import, sired 23 champions. Tarragona was the key dog in Rock Ridge Night Rocket's pedigree.
- Ch. Rock Ridge Night Rocket sired 36 champions.
- Ch. Power's Adventurer, a grandson of Night Rocket, sired 25 champions.
- Ch. Hughcliff Blue Tyler and Ch. Hughcliff Blue Tyson, tracing their pedigrees back to Night Rocket, produced 17 champions each.
- Ch. Canis Ida, the granddaughter of Tarragona, produced 7 champions.
- Eng. Am. Can. Ch. Fozzgyfurze Classic Cut, sired 17 champions, one of which was…
- Ch. Janice Blue Tango, producer of 7 champions.
- Cascadental Nemesis CD, grandaughter of Classic Cut, produced 8 champions.

With breeding of this caliber, it is no wonder that the Bedlington Terrier had a piece of the Terrier Group so often in the 1950s and 1960s.

THE 20TH CENTURY

In the last quarter of the 20th century, many breeders were active in the whelping box and the show ring, and new stars began to emerge on the scene.

John and Darlene Ready

John and Darlene Ready bred and showed Ch. Tiffanie's Spirit of America, a multiple all-breed Best in Show dog and a top producer of 15 champions, of which several are multiple group winners and Best in Show dogs.

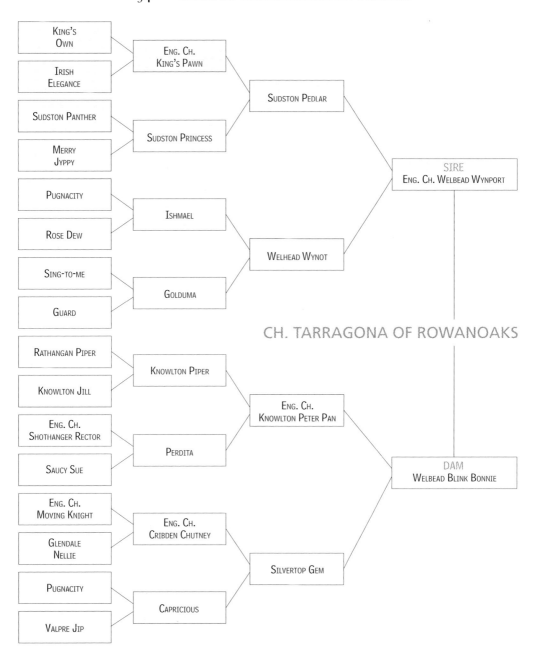

CH. TARRAGONA OF ROWANOAKS

Breeder: Mrs. R. J. Martin
Owner: Col. P. V. G. Mitchell

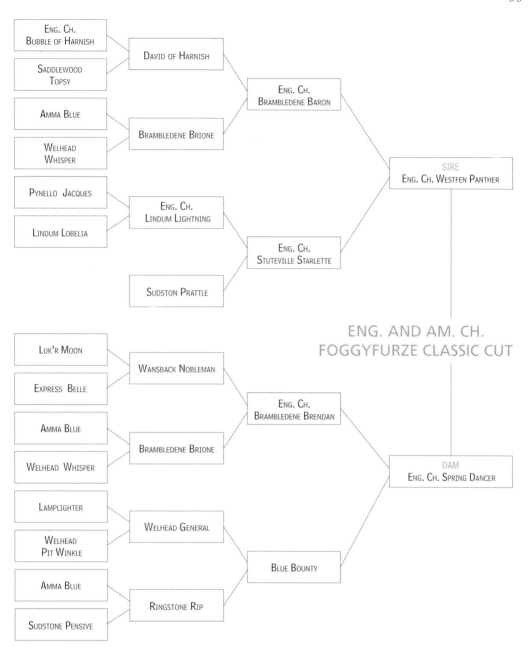

Eng. Ch. Bubble of Harnish	David of Harnish		
Saddlewood Topsy		Eng. Ch. Brambledene Baron	
Amma Blue	Brambledene Brione		
Welhead Whisper			SIRE Eng. Ch. Westfen Panther
Pynello Jacques	Eng. Ch. Lindum Lightning		
Lindum Lobelia		Eng. Ch. Stuteville Starlette	
Sudston Prattle			

ENG. AND AM. CH.
FOGGYFURZE CLASSIC CUT

Luk'r Moon	Wansback Nobleman		
Express Belle		Eng. Ch. Brambledene Brendan	
Amma Blue	Brambledene Brione		
Welhead Whisper			DAM Eng. Ch. Spring Dancer
Lamplighter	Welhead General		
Welhead Pit Winkle		Blue Bounty	
Amma Blue	Ringstone Rip		
Sudstone Pensive			

Breeder: N. Stead
Owner: L. H. Terpening

Frank Majocha of Barma Kennels with Ch. Barma Olympia Blaze.

Barma Kennels

Frank Majocha of Barma Kennels in Illinois bred and showed Ch. Barma Olympia Blaze, a multiple group winner and sire of seven champions. Altogether, 16 champions carried the Barma prefix. Frank was active throughout the 1980s and is a past president of the BTCA.

Don and Shirley Martin

In Canada, Don and Shirley Martin owned Can. Am. Ch. Siwash Blue Keeley, a multiple Best in Show winner.

Tamarack Kennels

Sally and Robert DeKold of Tamarack Kennels in Livonia, Michigan, have been active for many years in both the conformation and obedience rings. Sally has also been active in the BTCA.

OK Kennels

Jim and Marilyn O'Keefe of OK Kennels in Los Angeles had a number of champions, but the two standouts were Ch. OK's Rainbow of Rojo, sire of fifteen champions, and Ch. OK's Two Tone Quince, sire of ten champions, one of which was Ch. Merwyn's Percival Quiger, sire of eight champions.

Ch. OK's Rainbow of Rojo, sire of fifteen champions, winning Best of Breed in 1979. Pictured with handler/owner Jim O'Keefe, judge Grace Brewin, and trophy presenter Marjorie Hanson.

Ch. OK's Upsy Daisy of Vanole winning Group First. Owned by Jim O'Keefe. She is the dam of an all-champion litter of five.

Ch. OK's Tiny Tim winning Best of Breed at the 1968 Great Western Terrier Show. Owned and bred by Jim and Marilyn O'Keefe. He is the sire of eight champions.

Merwyn Kennels

Mary Squires had many champions from her Merwyn Kennels in the 1980s, including a top-producing bitch, Ch. Merwyn's Jennifer Fanger, dam of seven champions.

Flurry

Jerry and Dolores Schmidt from Wisconsin purchased their first Bedlington in the mid-1960s and bred under the Flury kennel name. Ch. Flurry's Rusty Jones was a specialty winner and had multigroup placements. In addition, they owned Am. Can. Ch. D'Argo Orion, an all-breed Best in Show winner, winner of five Chicago specialty shows, and Best of Breed at the 1976 BTCA Specialty in New York City. Jerry was a past president of the BTCA, and both were very active in the national club.

Am. Can. Ch. D'Argo's Orion, an all-breed Best in Show winner, winner of five Chicago Specialty shows, and Best of Breed at the 1976 BTCA New York Specialty. Shown here by owner Jerry Schmidt under breeder/judge Wilda Woehr.

Am. Can. Ch. D'Argo's Orion and Binker Hill's Kate Shelley winning Best of Breed and Best of Opposite Sex in 1976 with handlers Jerry Schmidt and Charles Pastorius.

Chrisandra Kennels

Sandra Christenson of Chrisandra Kennels in Milwaukee purchased her first Bedlington in 1969 and has bred many champions. Ch. Chrisandra's Fox Fire Vixen was bred to Ch. Binker Hill's Jumpin' Jubilee and had six puppies, of which five attained their championships. Ch. Chrisandra's Feisty Fox, co-owned with Marion Cabage, was a top-ten winner in 1972. Ch. Chrisandra's Foxy Leide, owned by Alan Sheimo and Marion Cabage, was Number One bitch in 1972, and Ch. Teaka's Sonny Too V Chrisandra, shown by Bobby Hutton and owned by Allan Sheimo and Basilo Bolumen, was Top Ten Bedlington in 1972. Chrisandra Fox Afire, used at stud only once, produced two champions, one of which was Ch. Willow Wind Flirtation, Number One Bedlington for three years. Sandra has also bred German Shorthaired Pointers and English

Ch. Chrisandra's Foxfire Vixen, dam of six champion offspring. Owned by Sandra Christenson.

Pointers over the years and wrote, "It took a while for me to get smart and get rid of the 'shedding' dogs. The Beds are definitely my favorite breed and an absolute joy to have."

Ch. Chrisandra's Eclipse, an excellent example from Chrisandra Kennels. Owned by Sandra Christenson.

Ch. Devonshire Tinker Toy finished his championship in 7 shows with 5 majors and 18 championship points. Owned by Rita Trish.

Rita Trish

Rita Trish has owned Bedlingtons since 1967 and has shown them in both conformation and obedience. All of her dogs have been titled in both areas. She is still the only Bedlington owner to have a champion Bedlington who was also a Utility Dog in obedience. She wrote about her current dog, Devonshire Tinker Toy ("Jellybean"), "I'm the owner, groomer, handler, and trainer, so I can tell you that Jellybean is the apple of my eye and he is spoiled rotten!" Rita has been a member of the BTCA for more than 30 years and has served on the board for 13 years.

Bobby Hutton

Bobby Hutton's most notable dog, which he bred, owned, and handled, was Ch. Sir Boychek Di Shepsel, who had 6 all-breed Bests in Show and was a top-producing sire with 13 champion get, most notable being Ch. Willow Wind Centurian, a great winning and producing Bedlington. Boychek was also the grandsire of the Best-in-Show dog, Ch. Bourbon's Apollo of Victoria.

Bobby Hutton, shown here handling Ch. Teaka's Sonny Too V Chrisandra, the Number One Bedlington in 1974.

Celin's Kennels

Jean and Howard Mathieu's Celin's Kennels have produced many champions, with the best-known being Ch. Celin's Cheyenne Raider, sire of 18 champions, owned by Sandy and Don Miles of Sandon Kennels in Georgia. Raider was Best of Breed at Westminster in 1975 and 1976 and a multiple specialty winner. His show career covered seven years and he was nearly always the Number-One Bedlington. Bred to Ch. Sandon's Blue Pebbles, he produced many champions, and Blue Pebbles herself was the dam of ten champions, a remarkable number for a bitch. Celin's Kennels had another top-producing male, Ch. Celin's Navajo Thunderbird, sire of 13 champions.

Willow Wind Kennels

David Ramsey of Willow Wind Kennels in Rhode Island has surely put his stamp upon the breed. Very active in Bedlingtons for more than 20 years, David became the consummate groomer and handler. Ch. Willow Wind Silver Cloud was the top Bedlington sire in 1980 and the sire of the top 1980 Bedlington, Ch. Lochmist Seashell. His double granddaughter, Ch. Willow Wind Social Butterfly, was the Number One Bedlington in 1983. Silver Cloud was intensively linebred, had a great "showdog attitude," and was the sire of 15 champions. Ch. Willow Wind Flirtation was an all-breed Best in Show and multiple specialty winning bitch, winning the BTCA 50th anniversary show. The great

Ch. Willow Wind's Flirtation, multiple all-breed Best in Show winner, Top Ten Bedlington for three years, and Best of Breed winner at the BTCA 50th Anniversary show. Owned by David Ramsey.

Ch. Willow Wind Centurian, top-winning Bedlington in breed history. Owned by David Ramsey, Mary Silkworth, Allan Sheimo.

dog, Ch. Willow Wind Centurian, sired by Ch. Sir Boychek Di Shepsel and out of an inbred Silver Cloud daughter, was the top-winning Bedlington in breed history. Best in Show at the Beverly Hills Kennel Club, he defeated more than 700 terriers in the Terrier Group. Centurian was co-owned with Mary Silkworth and Allan Sheimo. A Centurian daughter, Ch. Willow Wind Pardon Me Boys, co-owned with Maggie Rodenbach, was the Number Two Bedlington bitch in 1987. In the early 1990s, Ch. Willow Wind Play It My Way was a multiple all-breed Best in Show winner. David is no longer active in the breed, but there will probably be few that have made as much an impact upon the breed as he has.

Carillon Kennels

Lucy Heyman of Carillon Kennels in Texas became involved in the breed in the mid-1970s. To date, Lucy has shown many Bedlingtons to top wins. In addition, her daughter is also an

Am. Can. Ch. Willow Wind Got The Brass. Bred and owned by David Ramsey.

Jacquelyn Nicole Heyman, winning Best Junior Handler at the Denton Kennel Club in 1982 with Ch. Glen Valley's I Am Music, a Sonny Too son.

Ch. Carillon Salsa Serendipity is the all-time top producing dam with 16 champion get. She is a multiple Terrier Group Winner. Owned by Lucy Heyman.

accomplished handler. Ch. Claremont Lana, out of the last litter sired by Ch. Jolee Jingle Bells of Dovern, whelped in 1978, has over 100 champion descendants to date, including several top-ten dogs and multiple group winners. Ch. Carillon Salsa Serendipity is the all-time top-producing dam, with 16 champion get to her credit. Ch. Carillon Boulevardier was Number One Bedlington in 1997. Lucy has been very active in the breed, working particularly hard on compiling breed statistics and on the Bedlington hereditary problem of copper toxicosis. Lucy has provided particular assistance with the Bedlington statistics for this book.

Ch. Carillon Platinum Charlotte winning Best of Breed from the classes at the 1993 Houston Kennel Club National Specialty. Bred by Lucy Heyman.

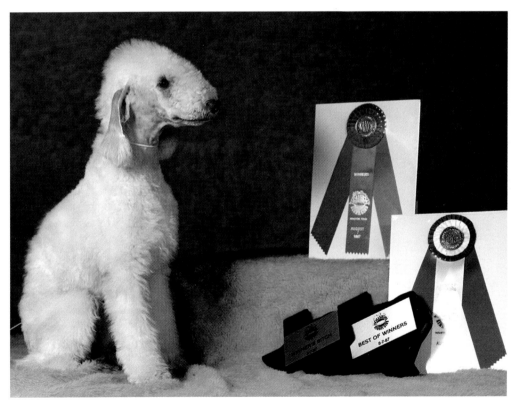

Ch. Magic Mist Molly Brown, littermate to top producer Ch. Magic Mist Sir Blue, CDX. Owned by Lucy Heyman.

Ch. Lochmist Cotton Candy, with handler Robert Wendel. Owned by Dolores Jean Jackson.

Cottonlane Kennels

Dolores Jean Jackson of Cottonlane Kennels in Nashville has been in the breed since 1977. Ch. Lochmist Cotton Candy was the Number One Bedlington bitch in 1983, won her first major at the Westminster Kennel Club show in 1982, and finished her championship with a five-point major over specials. Dolores also worked several Beds in working terrier trials. She noted that most terrier owners were surprised when a Bedlington showed up, because they "assumed one would not want their Bedlingtons going to ground and getting their pretty coats dirty in the underground tunnel."

Dolores Jean Jackson with Cotton Lane's Confection.

OTHER
BREEDERS

Other breeders who were active in the last 25 years of the 20th century included John and Donna Partenope of New Jersey. Their Ch. Jon Dee's Prince Charles was a top-ten Bedlington with multiple group wins. Both John and Donna were active in the BTCA. Karel Zadera of D'Argo Kennels in California produced many champions under his D'Argo prefix. Whirlwynd Kennels was the breeder of Ch. Whirlwynd's Winterhawk, sire of eleven champions, and Ch. Whirlwynd's Renegade, sire of twelve champions. Bob Bull's Binker Hills Kennel has produced many champions, and in addition, Bob is a very active board member of the BTCA and a winner of the Willemsen award. Bistry Kennels had two top-producing bitches, Ch. Bistry's Golden Touch, dam of seven champions, and Ch. Bistry's Graceful Ginger CD, dam of nine champions.

Time can only tell who the breeders of the future will be and who will have an impact on the breed to the extent that Rock Ridge, Firenze, and others have had. The breed is in good condition, and through the efforts and dedication of future breeders, it will remain so.

Bob Bull of Binker Hills Kennel bringing out a young Inverness puppy in 1975.

Ch. Binker Hill's Toast to Addie winning Best of Winners at the Montgomery County Kennel Club in 1977. Owned by Bob Bull.

Ch. Binker Hill's Kate Shelley. Bred by Helen Heintz.

Ch. Boulevardier Bad Leroy Brown, a top-winning Bedlington in Canada. Owned by Gail Gates and Elmer Grieve.

BEDLINGTON TERRIER SIRES WITH NINE OR MORE CHAMPION OFFSPRING

Ch. Willow Wind Centurian	50	Champions
Ch. Jolee Jingle Bells of Dovern	36	Champions
Ch. Rock Ridge Night Rocket	36	Champions
Ch. Gemar's Lord Jeffery	35	Champions
Ch. South Wind's Blue Velvet	32	Champions
Ch. Celin's Cheyenne Raider	25	Champions
Ch. Power's Adventurer	25	Champions
Ch. Carillon Boulevardier	23	Champions
Ch. Tarragona of Rowanoaks	23	Champions
Ch. Willow Wind Silver Cloud	23	Champions
Ch. Joker vom Bannwald	21	Champions
Ch. Gould's Top Flight of Valgo	21	Champions
Ch. Lucinda's Tim of Gold Grove	21	Champions
Ch. Tenby Toast	18	Champions
Ch. Foggyfurze Classic Cut	17	Champions
Ch. Hughcliff Blue Tyler	17	Champions
Ch. Hughcliff Blue Tyson	17	Champions
Ch. Turcott of Tartania	17	Champions
Ch. Magic Mist Sir Blue, CDX	16	Champions
Ch. OK's Rainbow of Rojo	15	Champions
Ch. Tiffanie's Spirit of America	15	Champions
Ch. Barma Sentinel O'Willow Wind	14	Champions
Ch. Doe Reen's Raymond Marvel	14	Champions
Ch. Ray's Smoky of Rowanoaks	14	Champions
Ch. Teaka's Sonny Too V Chrisandra	14	Champions
Ch. Albee's Admiration, CD	13	Champions
Ch. Celin's Navajo Thunderbird	13	Champions
Ch. D'Argo's Orion	13	Champions
Ch. Sir Boychek Di Shepsel	13	Champions
Ch. Liberty's Rain Beau Bleu	12	Champions
Ch. Cleo's Baron of Barrington	12	Champions
Ch. Royal Lancer of Tartania	12	Champions
Ch. Whirlwynd's Renegade	12	Champions
Ch. Hollywink Starcastle	11	Champions
Ch. Whirlwynd's Winterhawk	11	Champions
Ch. Willow Wind Family Jewels	11	Champions
Ch. Willow Wind Man About Town	11	Champions
Ch. Cathcade The Only One	10	Champions
Ch. Claremont Big Sur	10	Champions
Ch. Foggyfurze Ringostar	10	Champions
Ch. OK's Two Tone Quince	10	Champions
Ch. Singleton of Anderson Road	10	Champions
Ch. Touchwood Foolproof	10	Champions
Ch. Winphal's Silver Salute	10	Champions
Ch. Lord Oliver Cromwell	9	Champions

Note: Dogs with 9 to 16 champions are based on January 1969 through December 1999 *Gazette*.

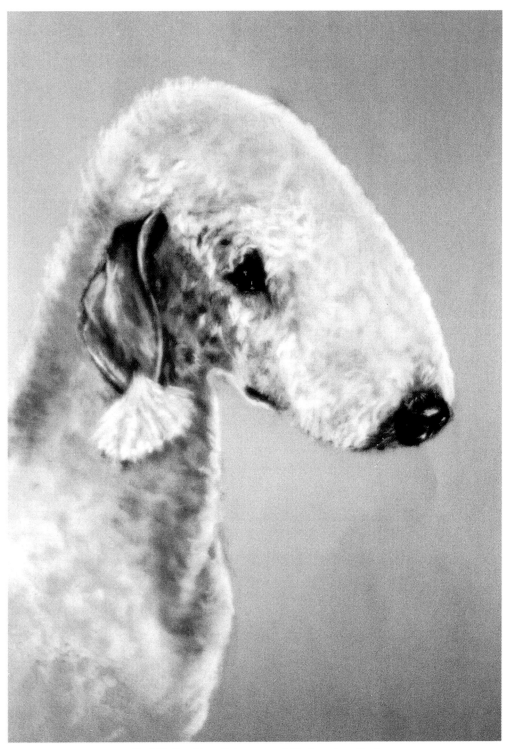

Ch. OK's Two Tone Quince, sire of 10 champion offspring.

Ch. Teaka's Sonny Too V Chrisandra, sire of 14 champion offspring.

Ch. Joker vom Bannwald, sire of 21 champion offspring.

Ch. Gemar's Lord Jeffrey, sire of 35 champion offspring.

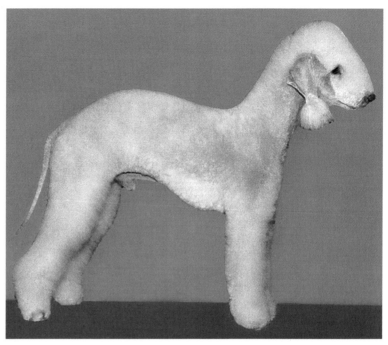

Am. Can. Ch. Carillon Boulvedarier, sire of 23 champion offspring.

Ch. Willow Wind Centurian, sire of 50 champion offspring.

BEDLINGTON TERRIER DAMS WITH SIX OR MORE CHAMPION OFFSPRING

Ch. Carillon Salsa Serendipity, CGC	16	Champions
Ch. Blue Angel of Tamarack	15	Champions
Ch. Misty Morn Chantilly Rose	14	Champions
Ch. Bo Peep's Blue Antonia	12	Champions
Ch. Elder's Bourbon	10	Champions
Ch. Sandon's Blue Pebbles	10	Champions
Ch. Touchwood Astra of Rowanoaks	10	Champions
Ch. Willow Wind Pardon Me Boys	10	Champions
Ch. Bistry's Graceful Ginger, CD	9	Champions
Ch. Conamor Lady Catherine	9	Champions
Ch. Marten's Bluebonnet of Bourbon	9	Champions
Silver Bede of Wetop	9	Champions
Su Beau's Blithe Spirit	9	Champions
Ch. Bourbon's Imposing Baiter	8	Champions
Ch. Carillon Serendipity	8	Champions
Cascadental Nemesis	8	Champions
Ch. Joben's Sparta of Homer	8	Champions
Ch. Merwyn Jennifer Fanger	8	Champions
Ch. Nettlecreek's Devil in Disquise	8	Champions
Ch. Touchwood Fool's Gold, CD	8	Champions
Albee Easter Parade	7	Champions
Ch. Bisty's Golden Touch	7	Champions
Ch. Canis Ida	7	Champions
Ch. Chelsea Blue, CD	7	Champions
Ch. Janice Blue Tango	7	Champions
Ch. Maid Melissa of Sherwood	7	Champion
Ch. Neary's Leedsagain	7	Champions
Ch. Oakhill 'n Sandon Sweet Deceit	7	Champions
South Wind's To 'n Fro of Sayles	7	Champions
Ch. Valgo's Whirlwind	7	Champions
Vansan's Red Pepper	7	Champions
Ch. Victoria's Image of Bourbon	7	Champions
Ch. Bridget Brown of Tiffany Hall	6	Champions
Ch. Bulaire Bonfire	6	Champions
Ch. Bulaire Firefly	6	Champions
Ch. Carillon Nova Stellarr	6	Champions
Ch. Cathcade Betty Blue	6	Champions
Ch. Chrisandra's Foxfire Vixen	6	Champions
Ch. Dyanna of Tartania	6	Champions
Ch. Foggyfurze Fondant	6	Champions
Ch. Fuzzi Logic Cache Controller	6	Champions
Ch. Fuzzi Logic Dynamic Link	6	Champions
Gould's Roslyn of Kenilworth, CD	6	Champions
Ch. Naughty Sadie of Pamper Hill	6	Champions
Ch. Robinglen Summer Romance	6	Champions
Shelbyshire Celin's Rollin' In	6	Champions
Ch. Tiffany of Rowanoaks	6	Champions
Ch. Touchwood Foolish Fancy	6	Champions
Ch. Touchwood Turtle Dove	6	Champions

Note: Dams with six champions are based on the January 1969 through December 1999 *Gazette*.

Ch. Carillon Salsa Serendipity, dam of 16 champion offspring.

Ch. Maid Melissa of Sherwood, dam of 7 champion offspring.

The Bedlington Terrier Club of America

⟋⟍

The Bedlington Terrier Club of America, a nonprofit organization, was recognized by the AKC in 1939.

As early as 1929, the Nearys were interested in forming a national club for the Bedlington. Thirty-five Bedlingtons were entered at the Morris and Essex show, held on May 29, 1932, and the 35 entries were owned by 14 different exhibitors (11 of the entries were brought by the Nearys). These exhibitors formed the nucleus of the new Bedlington club. Col. Guggenheim was elected president in absentia, Dr. McAnulty was secretary and treasurer, and Anna Neary was the vice president.

Mrs. Neary wrote about that May day and their trip to the show: "Let me take you in a taxi cab with eleven, that's right, *eleven* Bedlingtons; Neary driving and Exiled Laddie and Hasty Morn up front with him, two males and seven bitches riding with me. The Nearys were young and foolish and full of dreams! We arrived without incident. Incidentally, no crates, just collars and leashes. Alighting at the beautiful grounds of Giralda Farms (where the Morris and Essex show was held), the first object to greet our eyes was a lady with three Pekingese running loose. There was one thing Exiled Laddie had a deep aversion to—Pekingese! I don't remember how we got out of that encounter without ill effects. There were some runners around who grabbed some leashes. Others stood with raised eyebrows as we

The Bedlington Terrier Club of America 1967 New York Specialty, with judge Connie Willemsen and trophy presenter Adolph Kunca, BTCA President.

Chicago International Dog Show, 1966. Historical property of the Bedlington Terrier Club of America. *Donated by Claire Kilar*

untangled ourselves from the remaining leashes, wondering if we were some sort of nuts. On our return, Mrs. Harding asked us to take back her two males to New York City. It was fun for the onlookers to see 13 Bedlingtons and the loot getting into a taxi. On the long hot ride back, fortunately nothing went wrong, but as the old song says. 'I wouldn't do it now!'" Amid all of the turmoil, the Nearys still managed to get a Bedlington Terrier club off the ground.

The objectives of the BTCA are as follows:

* To encourage and promote the breeding of purebred Bedlington Terriers and to do all possible to bring their natural qualities to perfection.

* To insist that members and breeders accept the Standard of the Bedlington Terrier as adopted by the BTCA and approved by the American Kennel Club as the standard of excellence by which Bedlington Terriers shall be bred and judged.

* To conduct sanctioned and licensed specialty shows under the rules of the American Kennel Club.

* To urge all to follow the Code of Ethics adopted by the club as a guide for breeding, showing, and owning the Bedlington Terrier.

This photograph is from a BTCA meeting held in 1972, and includes President Adolph Kunca, Grace Brewin, and Connie Willemsen.

When you apply for membership in the BTCA, you will be asked to complete an application. In addition to the application and membership fee, you will also need the written sponsorship of an active BTCA member (this often will be the breeder of your dog).

After your membership is accepted, you will receive a packet of materials from the club secretary in addition to receiving the quarterly BTCA magazine, *Tassels and Tales.* The BTCA also has a Web site where you can download a membership application or keep track of recent show activities, complete with photographs. The address is http://clubs.akc.org/bcta/

The BTCA also has a very active rescue program, rescuing stray, abandoned, relinquished, and/or impounded Bedlingtons. Foster care is provided, with the eventual goal being the adoption and placement of the res-

Agatha, Steve Lasure's first Bedlington.

cued animal. Most dogs are spayed or neutered prior to placement. This is a well-thought-out program, run by dedicated individuals who want to see that all Bedlington Terriers have a loving and caring home. The program is supported by donations from individuals, and a donation is requested at the time a rescued dog is placed in his new home. It is very heartwarming to read the stories of these animals that had a poor start in life and then find themselves living in the warmth of a loving and caring family.

The Constance M. Willemsen Humanitarian Award is given each year to a member of the BTCA in recognition of the time and effort that he or she has put toward the Bedlington. This award is for an individual who displays sportsmanlike conduct at all times and who has been responsible for the advancement of the breed. Past Willemsen Award winners are Martha McVay, Jerry Schmidt, Dr. Ralph Roberts, Lois D'Ambrosio, and Robert Bull. Nominations for this award are made in writing by the membership, and the award is presented at the Montgomery County annual banquet in October.

There are two affiliate clubs for the Bedlington Terrier, the Bedlington Terrier Club of Greater Chicago and the Bedlington Terrier Club of the West, located in Southern California. Along with the national club, which holds its National Specialty at Ambler, Pennsylvania (Montgomery County Kennel Club), these two clubs offer specialty shows each year. The national club also sponsors a floating specialty that is held throughout the country every year.

The Constance M. Willemsen Humanitarian Award.

The Bedlington Terrier Club of America's 60th Anniversary, Montgomery County Kennel Club, 1997.

Within the BTCA, the membership includes those who are actively breeding and showing dogs, those who judge not only the Bedlington Terrier but all terriers and dogs in additional groups as well, and those who, year after year, work "doggedly" behind the scenes taking care of the club's business. The members are a wide range of people whose interest and love for the Bedlington bond them together, often forming lifelong friendships.

For information on the Bedlington Terrier Club of America or either of the affiliated clubs, write to the American Kennel Club at 51 Madison Avenue, New York, NY 10010 and they will send you the name, address, and e-mail of the current corresponding secretary. You may also get this information from the BTCA Web site at http://www.akc.org/clubs/btca.

At one time, many of the national terrier specialties were held in Rye, New York, in conjunction with the Rye Kennel Club, and the Bedlington Club was no exception. The show that was held in 1942, in the midst of the Second World War, had some interesting notes for club members: "The show special on the New Haven RR

New York BTCA Specialty, 1982—A happy group of fanciers.

Painted by Maude Earl, this reproduction is distributed only to the members of the Bedlington Terrier Club of America. This engraving is from the collection of Dr. and Mrs. Ralph Roberts, Evanston, Illinois.

leaves Grand Central Station on Sunday, June 7th, at 8:25 AM, arriving at Rye at 9:15 AM. Free trucking service from the Rye station to the show grounds (1/4 mile) and return will be provided. Dogs may be carried uncrated in the baggage car if supplied with suitable muzzles and leashes. If you have a car and can secure sufficient gas for the trip, take as many other exhibitors with you as possible."

The Neary Pin, although not given out by the BTCA, was the project of Anthony Neary, who always had his heart with the Bedlington and did everything he could to promote the breed. Mr. Neary made up the pins and awarded them to new exhibitors at the shows, from about 1955 to the early 1960s, ending at the time he was no longer able to attend shows because of illness. Mr. Neary gave the pins to exhibitors who were beginners at handling Bedlingtons. This was his way of rewarding the hours of preparation and dedication that the newcomer was putting into the breed.

PAST PRESIDENTS OF THE
BEDLINGTON TERRIER CLUB OF AMERICA

1932–? .... Col. M. Robert Guggenheim

193?–1935 .... Mrs. Emanuel Gerli

1936–1938 .... Sanford H. Freund

1939–1940 .... Col. P. V. G. Mitchell

1941-1946 .... Mrs. Rezin Davis

1947–1948 .... Mrs. Paul R. Willemsen

1949–1950 .... William A. Rockefeller

1951 .... Lewis H. Terpening

1952–1962 .... Commissioner Martin C. Epstein

1963–1973 .... Adolph F. Kunca

1974–1975 .... Raymond L. Herman

1976–1978 .... Mrs. Aquina Meyer

1979–1980 .... Ernest L. Matzner

1981–1983 .... Ronald H. Menaker

1984 .... Frank Majorca

1985 .... John Wood

1986–1988 .... Martha McVay

1989–1990 .... Jerry Schmidt

1991–1992 .... Ernest L. Matzner

1993–1999 .... Ralph Hogancamp

The Bedlington Terrier Standard

E ach breed approved by the American Kennel Club has a standard that gives the reader a mental picture of what the breed should look like. All reputable breeders strive to produce animals that will meet the requirements of the standard. Many breeds were developed for a specific purpose, such as hunting, retrieving, going to ground, coursing, guarding, herding, or working. The Bedlington Terrier, like the other terrier breeds, was bred to hunt the vermin and other rodents that were destructive to property.

Standards were originally written by fanciers who had a love and concern for the breed. They knew that the essential characteristics of the Bedlington Terrier were unlike any other breed and that care must be taken to maintain these characteristics through the generations.

As time progressed and breeders became more aware that certain areas of the dog needed a better description or more definition, breeders would meet together and work out a new standard. However, standards for any breed are never changed on a whim, and serious study and exchange between breeders takes place before any move is made. Anna Neary said, "Perhaps my eyes are blind with love of the Bedlington but I see no difference in the structure of today's Bedlingtons as compared with the earlier ones. His jacket is improved, and that is as it should be—even our own clothes have undergone quite a change from the 1890s!"

Head study of Ch. Gemar's Merri Kim. Owned by Gene McGuire.

The standard is continually studied by serious dog breeders and by judges. However, the reading and interpretation of the standard is subjective and open to interpretation by the individual who is reading it. It is important that every breeder and judge of Bedlington Terriers study the standard carefully in addition to seeing as many Bedlington Terriers as possible. Through time and study, a picture will form in the mind of what constitutes a correct Bedlington.

The present standard, as revised by the BTCA membership and approved by the American Kennel Club, is as follows:

General Appearance—A graceful, lithe, well-balanced dog with no sign of coarseness, weakness, or shelliness. In repose the expression is mild and gentle, not shy or nervous. Aroused, the dog is particularly alert and full of immense energy and courage. Noteworthy for endurance, Bedlingtons also gallop at great speed, as their body outline clearly shows.

Head—Narrow, but deep and rounded. Shorter in skull and longer in jaw. Covered with a profuse topknot which is lighter than the color of the body, highest at the crown, and tapering gradually to just back of the nose. There must be no stop and the unbroken line from crown to nose end reveals a slender head without cheekiness or snipiness. Lips are black in the blue and blue and tans and brown in all other solid and bi-colors.

Eyes—Almond-shaped, small, bright and well sunk with no tendency to tear or water. Set is oblique and fairly high on the head. Blues have dark eyes; blues and tans, less dark with amber lights; sandies, sandies and tans, light hazel; livers, livers and tans, slightly darker. Eye rims are black in the blues and blue and tans, and brown in all other solid and bi-colors.

Ears—Triangular with rounded tips. Set on low and hanging flat to the cheek in front with a slight projection at the base. Point of greatest width approximately 3 inches. Ear tips reach the corners of the mouth. Thin and velvety in texture, covered with fine hair forming a small silky tassel at the tip.

Nose—Nostrils large and well-defined. Blues and blues and tans have black noses. Livers, livers and tans, sandies, sandies and tans have brown noses.

Jaws—Long and tapering. Strong muzzle well filled up with bone beneath the eye. Close-fitting lips, no flews.

Teeth—Large, strong and white. Level or scissors bite. Lower canines clasp the outer surface of the upper gum just in front of the upper canines. Upper premolars and molars lie outside those of the lower jaw.

Neck and Shoulders—Long, tapering neck with no throatiness, deep at the base and rising well up from the shoulders which are flat and sloping with no excessive musculature. The head is carried high.

Body—Muscular and markedly flexible. Chest deep. Flat-ribbed and deep through the brisket, which reaches to the elbows. Back has a good natural arch over the loin, creating a definite tuck-up of the underline. Body slightly greater in length than height. Well-muscled quarters are also fine and graceful.

Legs and Feet—Lithe and muscular. The hind legs are longer than the forelegs, which are straight and wider apart at the chest than at the feet. Slight bend to pasterns, which are long and sloping without weakness. Stifles well angulated. Hocks strong and well let down, turning neither in nor out. Long hare feet with thick, well-closed-up, smooth pads. Dewclaws should be removed.

Coat—A very distinctive mixture of hard and soft hair standing well out from the skin. Crisp to the touch but not wiry, having a tendency to curl, especially on the head and face. When in show trim must not exceed one inch on body; hair on legs is slightly longer.

The Bedlington should give the impression of a muscular, game, and athletic terrier. Ch. Capstone One Over Par. Owned by Charla Hill and Mike Sanders.

Tail—Set low, scimitar-shaped, thick at the root and tapering to a point which reaches the hock. Not carried over the back or tight to the underbody.

Color—Blue, sandy, liver, blue and tan, sandy and tan, liver and tan. In bi-colors the tan markings are found on the legs, chest, under the tail, inside the hindquarters and over each eye. The topknots of all adults should be lighter than the body color. Patches of darker hair from an injury are not objectionable, as these are only temporary. Darker body pigmentation of all colors is to be encouraged.

Height—The preferred Bedlington Terrier dog measures $16\frac{1}{2}$ inches at the withers, the bitch $15\frac{1}{2}$ inches. Under 16 inches or over $17\frac{1}{2}$ inches for dog and under 15 inches or over $16\frac{1}{2}$ inches for bitches are serious faults. Only where comparative superiority of a specimen outside these ranges clearly justifies it, should greater latitude be taken.

Weight—To be proportionate to height within the range of 17 to 23 pounds.

Gait—Unique lightness of movement. Springy in the slower paces, not stilted or hackneyed. Must not cross, weave or paddle.

Approved September 12, 1967

The Bedlington has a very distinctive coat, consisting of a mixture of hard and soft hair standing well out from the skin. Am. Can. Ch. Chimneyhouse Bobby Dazzler. Owned by Vicki Petris.

Illustrated Standard for the Bedlington Terrier

GENERAL APPEARANCE

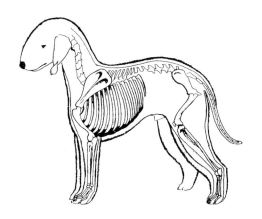

CORRECT

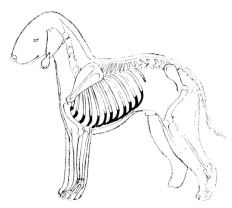

INCORRECT

Short Round Ribs

CORRECT

INCORRECT

Round Eye
Heavy Head
Heavy Bone
Round Rib
Fluffy Coat

Illustrated Standard for the Bedlington Terrier

HEAD

CORRECT

NARROW
Snipey

INCORRECT
Cheeky

CORRECT PROFILE

INCORRECT PROFILE
Short Foreface
Wide Ear

CORRECT PROFILE

INCORRECT PROFILE
Short Foreface
Short Ear
Large Round Eye

Illustrated Standard for the Bedlington Terrier

EYES

CORRECT EYE

INCORRECT EYE

Round

Illustrated Standard for the Bedlington Terrier

EARS

CORRECT EAR

HIGH EAR SET

SHORT WIDE EAR

NARROW EAR

STRAIGHT SET ON

Illustrated Standard for the Bedlington Terrier

NOSE

Illustrated Standard for the Bedlington Terrier

TEETH

CORRECT

Scissors Bite

INCORRECT

Overshot

CORRECT

Level Bite

INCORRECT

Undershot

Illustrated Standard for the Bedlington Terrier

NECK AND SHOULDERS

CORRECT
Well Laid Back Shoulder

INCORRECT
Forward Shoulder

CORRECT NECK

INCORRECT
Short Thick Neck

INCORRECT
Ewe Neck

INCORRECT
Straight Up Neck

Illustrated Standard for the Bedlington Terrier

BODY

GOOD BEDLINGTON RIB CAGE   ROUND RIB CAGE

Front View   Incorrect in a Bedlington

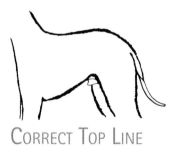

CORRECT TOP LINE   FLAT BACK

SWAY BACK—HIGH RUMP

Illustrated Standard for the Bedlington Terrier

LEGS AND FEET

FRONT VIEW
of
Well Arched Toes

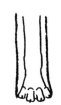

INCORRECT
Splayed Foot

CORRECT
Hare Foot

INCORRECT
Round (Cat-Foot)

CORRECT
FRONT

TOEING OUT

TOEING IN

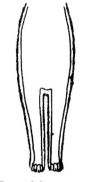

TOO NARROW

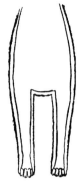

TOO WIDE

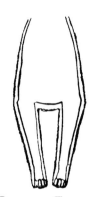

OUT AT ELBOWS

Illustrated Standard for the Bedlington Terrier

LEGS AND FEET

WELL LET DOWN
Low Hocks

HIGH HOCKS

CORRECT PAD
Oval

INCORRECT PAD
Round-Cat Foot

CORRECT

INCORRECT
Toeing In Hocks Out

INCORRECT
Toeing Out Cow Hocked

Illustrated Standard for the Bedlington Terrier

TAIL

CORRECT
Low Set Tail

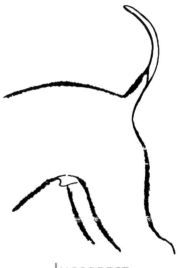

INCORRECT
High Set Gay Tail

HIGH TAIL

TUCKED UNDER

Illustrated Standard for the Bedlington Terrier

GAIT

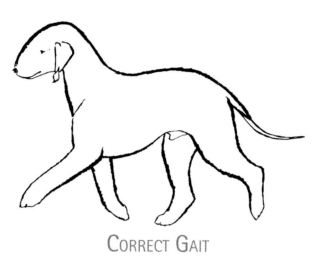

CORRECT GAIT

INCORRECT
Hackney Gait

Illustrated Standard for the Bedlington Terrier

GAIT

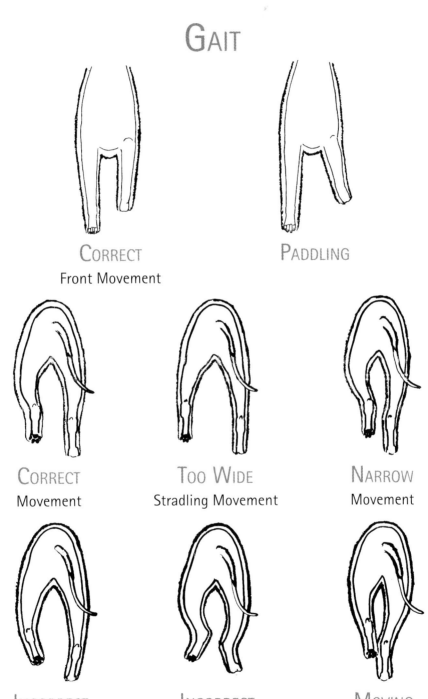

CORRECT
Front Movement

PADDLING

CORRECT
Movement

TOO WIDE
Stradling Movement

NARROW
Movement

INCORRECT
Toeing in Movement

INCORRECT
Cow Hocked Movement

MOVING
Close and Crossing

COAT COLOR   The breed standard notes that the coat colors of Bedlingtons are as follows: blue, sandy, liver, blue and tan, sandy and tan, liver and tan, and bi-colors. The most common color, however, is blue, with liver following second. Puppies are born black, chocolate brown, or dark coffee, and within the first year of life they will mature into the adult color. The mature Bedlington coat can periodically vary from light to dark.

Color inheritance and the genetic factors that make up color inheritance can be complicated to the nonscientific mind. The Bedlington breeder, Elisabeth (E. M. J.) Funkhouser (a zoology major and breeder from the 1940s and '50s) wrote an article for *Leash and Collar* that explains coat color inheritance in layman terms:

"The inheritance of color is really very simple and it works. The important thing is to understand that every animal gets two factors for anything it inherits: one from the father and one from the mother. If the father is pure blue and the mother is also pure blue, the offspring will be pure blue also as it received a blue factor from each parent. However, if the father is pure blue and the mother is pure liver, each offspring will receive one factor for blue and one factor for liver. These

A blue-colored Bedlington puppy, Lochmist Summer Snowcone. Owned by Dolores Jean Jackson.

A blue and tan litter bred by Jim and Marilyn O'Keefe. All became champions.

offspring would appear blue, just like the blue parent, because in dogs the blue is dominant to liver. However, the liver is actually there temporarily hidden but still potent. If two puppies from a litter sired by a pure blue dog out of a pure liver bitch are mated together, this hidden liver factor will show itself in a ratio of one liver to three blues in the resulting litter. Of the three blues, one would be a pure blue and two would be hybrid blues, like the parents. It should be noted that all livers are pure in that they cannot carry blue. But blues can be either pure blue or hybrid blue (carrying liver recessively). A blue Bedlington is either pure blue or else half (hybrid) blue. If a liver turns up from a long line of blue ancestors, then that color has been carried down in recessive form right from that distant liver in the pedigree of each parent. And such a liver is

Colors within a litter can vary. One blue and three liver-colored Carillon Bedlingtons. Owned by Lucy Heyman and Dr. Cynthia Cook.

just as much a pure liver as one from liver parents. Livers bred together can produce nothing but liver puppies, of course.

"In understanding the inheritance of blue and tan, one must realize that this is transmitted quite independently of the blue-liver factors. It is easier to deal with the 'and tan' pattern if we call it bicolor, as it can affect either blues or livers, and consider it in opposition to solid color. Blue and tan then becomes blue bicolor and liver and tan (that rare color) is liver bicolor. Bicolor, then, is recessive to solid colors, no matter which color you deal with.

"As an example of complex heredity, if you mated a pure solid liver to a pure blue and tan, you would get nothing but solid blue puppies! This is because solid covers the bicolor in all the puppies and blue covers up the liver in all of them. The fact that these dominant factors come from different parents makes no difference. It would be just the same as mating a pure solid blue to a pure liver and tan."

Purchasing Your Bedlington Terrier

⌒w⌒

I t must be remembered that when you purchase a pet, whether a cat or a dog, the animal will become a part of your family and will be with you for many years. Unlike your brothers or sisters, when you elect to bring home a pet you get to select the one that you think will fit into the family the best and that will be a welcomed addition to your family's style of living.

Buying a dog should require some study and time. Do not rush out to the pet shop and bring home the dog that looks the neediest or go to your neighbor who breeds her bitch every six months to the male down the block. Do not bring home a puppy that grows into a 100-pound dog and no longer fits into your two-room apartment. And for heaven's sake, do not buy the puppy that hangs back in the box because you feel sorry for him. When you add this member to the family, take a good look at what you are buying and make certain that it is what your family wants and needs.

Consider the purchase of your dog to be a major purchase. You may take six months or so to select your new car or a large appliance. Take at least that long to select your dog. You may have the car for 5 years, but your puppy will be a family member for much longer—probably at least 8 years and maybe as much as 12 or 14 years. And as they say, having a dog is just like having a child, except he never grows up.

First, stop at your local library or bookstore and pick up one book about dogs in general and one on the terriers in particular. The next step that you should take is to attend a local all-breed dog show and watch the Bedlington judging. Look over your catalog

and see who the breeders are and which kennels the winners are coming from. After the judging, talk to these breeders and ask any questions that you still have in regard to Bedlington ownership.

Throughout this book, we have referred to "reputable" breeders. A reputable breeder is one who is devoted to making certain that you and the Bedlington are suited to each other. He will want to know that you will offer a good home life, including a fenced-in yard and the attention and love that the dog will need.

BTCA President Ralph Hogancamp with an armful of Bedlington love.

A reputable breeder has carefully selected his breeding animals and is continually striving to produce better dogs. He has checked the health of his puppies, wormed them, given them their shots, and done his best not to have bred in any genetic problems. A

A reputable breeder will only breed the best dogs to ensure the health and quality of the pups produced. This 10-week-old litter, bred by Gene McGuire, all became champions before 16 months of age.

It is extremely hard to resist an adorable Bedlington puppy, but make sure you have carefully considered the responsibilities of dog ownership before bringing one home. Puppies bred by Lucy Heyman and Dr. Cynthia Cook.

reputable breeder will sell you a Bedlington that looks like a Bedlington and has the proper Bedlington temperament.

The breeder will belong to a local all-breed club and the national club. Do not hesitate to ask the breeder which organizations he belongs to, how active he has been, and how long he has been a member.

When you visit a kennel, look around to see if it is clean and cared for. The yard should be clean, the kennel area well lit, and the puppies fat and happy. They should enjoy seeing a stranger and not cower in a corner. The breeder should show you the dam of the litter, and if the sire is on the premises, you should see him, too. These dogs should be in good condition, with shiny coats and good temperaments.

If you are interested in purchasing a Bedlington puppy, ask the BTCA or local breed club to help you find a reputable breeder in your area. Ch. Capstone One Under Par with breeder/owner Michael D. Sanders.

A reputable breeder may not have a puppy for you when you are ready to buy one. Often, breeders only have one or two litters a year, and you may have to wait until the next breeding. A reputable breeder will not push a six-week-old puppy on you, but will keep the pup until he is eight or ten weeks old and ready to leave the nest. Just be patient and the right puppy will come your way.

Give some consideration as to whether you want a male or a female. A female will come into season every six months or so, unless you have her spayed. Females seem to mature more quickly than the males, and with their first season they quickly become young ladies and lose some of their "puppy giggles." Males can remain like rambunctious teenagers for a long time.

Do not close your mind to an older dog. Some breeders will have a two- or three-year-old that they would like to place—perhaps the dog has finished his championship and there is no longer a place in the breeder's program for him. Or perhaps they need to move an older dog on to make room for a promising puppy. There are many advantages to this. The dog is mature, he is often housetrained, and if not, he is a quick learner. The mature dog will not chew the rugs and will be well socialized. In 1995, we added a four-year-old champion French Bulldog to our household and have found him a delight in every way.

If you do not have the time or inclination to train a puppy, an adult Bedlington can make a wonderful addition to your family. Rachel and Paige Pruitt with their Bedlington friends.

Whether you bring home a show-quality or pet-quality Bedlington, he will become a cherished companion for many years to come. Cotton Lane's Confection, owned by Dolores Jean Jackson.

With training and care, who knows how far your Bedlington puppy can go? This nine-week-old puppy, owned by Helen Heintz, grew up to be Ch. Inverness Paige.

Do not buy your dog from a puppy mill—individuals who may be breeding as many as 100 dogs of various breeds. You may pay as much for the dog as you would from a reputable breeder, and you will probably end up with a dog that doesn't look very much like a Bedlington and that could well be sickly on top of it.

If you are a first-time Bedlington owner and have never shown a dog, do expect the breeder to sell you a good dog with a good pedigree, but do not expect that you will receive an animal that will go Best in Show his first time out. It's always possible, of course, just as winning the lottery is possible, and your chances will be just about the same. You are looking for a pet, a family member. And for your first dog, that is just what the breeder will sell you—a well-bred, healthy, well-adjusted Bedlington Terrier that your family will enjoy for many years.

Breeding Your Bedlington Terrier

⌒ℳ⌒

S everal thoughts should be kept in mind when you consider breeding your bitch:

- Not every bitch needs to be bred. Take a look at your local animal shelter and see the numbers of unwanted dogs that will eventually be put down for lack of a home.

- Do not breed your bitch because you want your children to see "Mother Nature at work." There are good videos at the library that can answer their questions.

- Do not breed your bitch because you want to "make some money." It's just about impossible to make any money on a litter and, in general, it will be a losing operation.

- Do not breed your bitch because you think "one litter will be good for her." Is a woman "better" because she goes through childbirth?

Think about the following before taking on the responsibility of a litter of puppies:

- A litter of puppies is very time-consuming. You and the rest of the family will be spending hours with the puppies, cleaning them, worrying over them, and socializing them.

- A litter of puppies is very hard on the house. Rugs are not only soiled but they are often chewed around the corners, as is the woodwork and furniture. Once outside, the pups can create havoc in the yard.

- A litter of puppies will cost you money. First, you have a stud fee. Then, your bitch has a possibility of requiring a cesarean section, which is a substantial expense. Your puppies will require shots, a big expense if you have a large litter. The Bedlington Terrier also requires the removal of the dewclaws on the third day, another veterinary expense.
- You can't count on selling your puppies quickly. You may have one or two pups with you until six months of age or more. In the meantime, the family becomes attached to them, your dog food bills continue to rise, and your patience runs thin.

If you do decide to breed, answer the following questions:

- Is your bitch of quality? Does she have a good pedigree, linebred with a championship background? (One champion out of 64 descendants does not make a championship background.) Did you talk to the breeder that you bought your bitch from in regard to breeding her? Did she tell you that you should breed your girl or did she sell her to you as a pet?
- Which stud dog should you breed to? Ask your breeder for her opinion. Use a dog that has a solid pedigree—not only a championship background, but a champion and possibly a group or Best in Show winner himself. The stud fee will not be much more than breeding to a mediocre dog.
- When should you have this litter? Spring and summer litters are easier than fall and winter litters because you can have the puppies outside more. Do you have a big vacation planned for the summer?
- Is there any interest in Bedlington puppies in your area? Ask the reputable breeder, the one with the stud dog that is being used, and she can tell you.

A note in regard to reputable, experienced breeders: These are the individuals who have been breeding Bedlingtons for 10, 20, or more years. They belong to an all-breed club and to the BTCA. They show their dogs, attend the national shows, and keep abreast of the trends in the breed. A wise newcomer will build upon their experience. Don't think that you can come along and breed a "star" with a pet shop bitch. This happens about as often as lightning striking the same place twice. And remember, always start with a quality bitch. You probably won't live long enough to breed up to the quality of the big winners of the day unless you start with quality.

Even if you have decided that you have a quality dog that should be bred and you are going ahead with this project, you have talked to the breeder of your bitch and it's determined that you should breed her, and you have found a good stud dog and are ready to get to work, there is still much to learn.

A Bedlington bitch will come into season the first time when she is around eight to ten months old and again approximately every six months after that. Do not breed your bitch the first season. Wait until she is around 18 months old and then consider breeding her.

You should contact the owner of the stud dog that you have selected when you first notice that your bitch is in season. You will be told when to bring or ship her to the kennels so that she can be bred sometime between the 11th and 15th days of her estrus.

Breeding should only be attempted by those that have the knowledge, facilities, time, and money to care for the mother and all of the resulting puppies. Ten-week-old Bedlingtons bred by Gene McGuire and Gretchen Ochs.

Once your dog has been bred, by the sixth week of gestation (gestation for dogs is 63 days) you should know if she is pregnant. Decide which room will be the nursery, making sure that you have picked a quiet spot out of the hubbub of daily living. Sometimes you can borrow a whelping box from another breeder, otherwise a box can

Pregnant mothers need lots of special care and extra attention.

be easily made. A wooden box is nice, a wire kennel can be excellent, and a cardboard box is acceptable. The pen should be about 3 by 3 feet and about 8 to 12 inches high. A guard rail (also called a "pig rail") should be placed around the inside of the box, approximately 3 inches above the ground. This gives the puppies an area to crawl under for protection against the mother's weight when she leans against the side of the box.

Start taking her temperature with a rectal thermometer about the 59th day after the first breeding. A dog's temperature averages about 101.5 degrees, and as the whelping becomes more imminent, the temperature will start to drop. When it settles down to 98 degrees or so, you should be expecting pups within 24 hours. During these days you will also note a sticky and smelly discharge from the vulva, and by now your girl should be quite heavy and may need assistance with the steps. Hold her on your lap and you can feel the puppies moving around.

You can expect between two and five puppies in your litter. Puppies delivered naturally will usually be delivered anywhere from 20-minute to 3-hour intervals. It's a good idea when the first puppy is delivered to note the time of day, sex, and color of the puppy on a notepad. If you should have a long delay between births, you will have specific information to give your veterinarian if you need to call for assistance.

Puppies are born in a sac to which they are attached by the umbilical cord. Do not break this sac as the pup is emerging from the birth canal. Have patience, because it can take up to ten minutes before the pup in the sac "pops" out. When the pup comes out, the mother should reach around, open the sac, and snip off the umbilical cord with her teeth. At this point, however, many breeders take matters into their own hands and will cut the umbilical cord with clean scissors and tie it off about two inches from the tummy. Again, most breeders, at this point, help the mother by rubbing the puppy dry with a clean, terrycloth towel until they hear a good, healthy cry

Puppies are born in a sac attached to the umbilical cord, which the mother will remove.

from the pup. While doing this, look the puppy over and make sure that everything appears to be in order. Now you are ready to hand this fellow over to the mother, and she will wash it all over again and pull the pup up to her nipples.

Puppies and bitch should be kept in a draft-free, warm area. Take the mother outside after the whelping is completed and let her relieve herself. Clean up her rear end, put down clean towels or rugs in the box, and make her a dish of soft food. Give this to her along with a pan of water.

A special note about the color of Bedlington puppies: The blues are born black and the livers and sandies are born brown. Blue and tans, as well as liver and tans, distinctly show the two colors. It is perfectly all right for the puppies to have some white markings in their puppy coat colors.

Puppies and mother relax and bond after birth. Puppies should be kept in a draft-free, warm area.

RAISING A HEALTHY LITTER

The first five days of your puppies' lives are the most important ones.

You can do some simple things to help ensure healthy puppies: Keep the whelping box and the puppies in a draft-free area; keep the temperature in the whelping room at a minimum of 75 degrees; and see that your mother is staying healthy, eating well, and drinking water.

When you look in your whelping box, you should see a contented mother and litter. Your mother should be eating well, drinking water, and giving off an air of well-being. The puppies should be tucked up around her, alternately sleeping and nursing. They should be quiet, happy, and warm.

Watch for the following trouble signs: body temperature drop, no weight gain, dehydration. Check for dehydration by pinching the skin. On a healthy pup, the skin pops back into place; on a dehydrated pup, the skin stays pinched. If your mother appears listless or if your whole litter starts crying, you have a problem. Call your veterinarian and tell him that you are bringing your bitch in, and ask him if he also wants to see the puppies.

Remember this when raising a litter: Most litters are healthy litters. Your puppies will usually survive and your mothers will usually be attentive and healthy. You should do whatever you can to ensure that this is the case. Keep your whelping pen clean—an easy job for the first two weeks or so, as the mother does most of the work. Feed your mother properly. If it is a large litter, you will probably have to increase her food, feeding her several times a day when the pups are approximately three weeks old. Look each puppy over every day and make sure that everything is functioning. Talk to your veterinarian about having the dewclaws removed three days after their birth.

For the first few weeks of life, puppies receive antibodies through nursing that will protect them from disease. After that period of time, they will need to begin a vaccination schedule.

Although most litters are healthy, pups do die, no matter how you might try and save them. Here is a general rule of thumb: A cold puppy is a dead puppy. A puppy that the mother persistently ignores and pushes to the side of the pen will usually be a dead puppy within a matter of hours. Something is wrong with the pup and the mother knows it. Use your discretion about how much you want to do to save this kind of puppy.

Start weaning your litter between three and five weeks. The larger the litter, the more important it is to start weaning early to help their mother with the feedings. When you start to wean your

Newborn puppies are very vulnerable, and the breeder needs to provide extra care to keep them healthy.

A breeder will start his or her Bedlington pups on a healthy diet. Once the puppies are weaned, they can begin eating a soft puppy kibble.

puppies, mix up a gruel of high-quality puppy kibble. Make a very mushy meal with no lumps in it. At the time you start to feed your pups, offer them a pan of water also. As the pups start to eat more on their own and as their teeth start to come in, the mother will become less and less interested in spending time with the pups.

When the puppies are between five and eight weeks old, take them to your veterinarian for their shots. Your vet will tell you when to bring your pups in, which shots they should have, and how many times they need to be repeated. At this time, you should also take in a stool sample for analysis. If your pups are wormy, your veterinarian will give you the proper medication to clear up the worms.

By now you should have trimmed the puppies' toenails several times. It is now time to start setting up each puppy on the grooming table and wiping them down with a damp cloth. It is never too early to get them used to being handled and groomed. Be sure to put their head in the noose and do not leave them unattended at any time. Turn on your clipper and place it beside the dog's neck so that he gets used to the vibrations and the sound. You do not need to trim at this time, just get the pup accustomed to the feel of the clipper.

Between 8 and 12 weeks of age, the Bedlington puppy can go to his new home. The good care that the breeder has provided will be reflected in a Bedlington's health and well-being.

Decide how long you want to keep your pups before placing them in a home. A pup should never go to a new home before 8 weeks of age, and many breeders like to keep them until 12 weeks. When the pup goes to his new home, have him clean and smelling good. Give the new owner a list of the foods that you use and note the number of times a day that you are feeding him. Give him the name of a veterinarian in his area. It's nice to add a little breed book and a leash, too. Of course, send the registration papers and a copy of the pedigree.

With your first litter, it may be hard to see the rascals go off to a new home. However, keep in mind that it is rather nice to have one of these little bundles that you have spent so much time on go off into his own little world and be appreciated and loved by others.

Health

For the most part, the Bedlington is considered to be a healthy breed, with no more genetic or health problems than most breeds. Give your dog care, use your common sense, and have a good veterinarian available. Take your dog to the vet when you think you have a problem, follow instructions, and recovery will usually be very rapid.

Your dog should have yearly inoculations along with a stool sample test to make certain that he is free from worms. Keep the teeth clean and the nails trimmed. Your veterinarian can do these jobs if you or your groomer are unable to do so. Watch for ticks in the summer and clean out any wounds. Some wounds may require veterinary care. Yearly heartworm checks are also important in some areas of the country.

Keep your dog groomed and clean. Watch the ears for ear mites or other infections. Watch your dog in the summer heat, keep him out of the sun, and certainly don't ever leave him in the car on a warm day.

If your veterinarian is not available at odd hours for emergencies, know where the emergency veterinarian is located and keep the telephone number handy. Many veterinarians in large cities no longer have an emergency service, and you must rely on these special facilities for late evening, weekend, and holiday service.

A Bedlington puppy will have a good start in life if his dam and sire are healthy and well adjusted. Ch. Von's Bramble Buddy with son Bramble's Charles Lord O' Lake. Owned by Paula Von Gerichten.

Your dog should be kept in either a fenced yard or on a leash. It's foolish, and often against the law, to let your dog run loose and take a chance of him being run over by a car. Too often the story is heard about the dog living at the end of the cul-de-sac where only one delivery truck comes along a day—and that truck runs over the dog. It only takes one vehicle to shorten a dog's life.

Dogs often live to seven or eight years and then die of some disease, although terriers do have a tendency to live longer than many other breeds. Eleven and 12-year-old Bedlingtons are not unusual, and often the terriers live to 15 or 16 years old. Remember, anything after eight years of age, in any breed, is considered to be a gift.

Cancer diagnosis can happen in any breed of dog, and Bedlingtons are no exception. As in man, there is not always a cure and again, as in man, early detection is your best form of prevention. Check your dog over each time you groom him for any lumps or bumps that you have not noticed before. Fast-growing lumps are cause for concern, particularly when found around the mammary glands. Your veterinarian should check any lump that you do not like the look of or that is growing rapidly.

As your dog ages, he may require special care. Regular veterinary checkups, preventative health maintenance, a good diet, and lots of love can keep your Bedlington happy and comfortable from puppyhood throughout his senior years.

COPPER TOXICOSIS

The Bedlington Terrier can have a particular genetic disease called copper toxicosis. This is an autosomal recessive disorder of copper accumulation that results in severe liver disease. It is a hereditary condition and one that cannot be ignored. Considerable research and study, particularly with the Bedlington, has been done. When buying your puppy, be sure to ask the breeder to see the certificates of normal biopsies of both the sire and dam. All responsible Bedlington breeders will have their dogs certified normal before breeding them. It is thought that the disease may be in as much as half of the breed—however, there was a time when two-thirds of the breed was affected. If your dog is diagnosed with the disease, there are now several therapies that he can undergo and often live a long and full life.

THE GERIATRIC DOG

The geriatric dog—one over eight years of age—may require a little more or different care than the younger dog. As your dog ages, he will slow down and possibly suffer arthritis to varying degrees. His sight and hearing may start waning, and he may sleep more. Let him have his way. Do not expect him to do the three-mile walk as he did as a pup. You may want to try dog food for the geriatric or

Responsible breeders will screen all of their Bedlingtons for genetic diseases before breeding them to ensure the health of the future offspring.

sedate dog. Be sure he has a warm space to sleep and try to keep him at a normal weight, as excess weight can be difficult on the joints.

As he ages and becomes more infirm, you will eventually be faced with the decision to "put your dog down." Unfortunately, dogs and humans do not die peacefully in their sleep very often. With the dog, we are able to make a decision to be a humane owner, and the day may come when you take your pet in to be euthanized by your veterinarian. It's hard to know when it's time, but again, use your common sense and try not to let your dog suffer unduly. Your veterinarian will administer a very quick drug, and you will be surprised how quickly and peacefully he will die in your arms. This is a terribly sad day for the entire family, but it often takes only a few weeks or months before you are off looking for your new Bedlington Terrier.

Grooming the Bedlington Terrier

D o understand before purchasing your Bedlington Terrier that this is a breed with a coat that needs maintenance, whether you have a dog for the show ring or a household pet. Think of it in the same terms as your child—you bathe your youngster, comb his hair, and put a clean set of clothes on him. The result is that you have a child that smells good, looks nice, and is a pleasure to be around. It is the same with your dog—keep the dog brushed, cleaned, and trimmed, and you will enjoy his company. However, this will require some effort.

The Bedlington has a nonshedding coat that requires the removal of dead hair. Left untended, the coat will become matted and eventually smelly. A weekly or twice-a-week combing will take out the dead hair, and it is unlikely that you will have a matted coat. Whether you have a show dog or a pet, trimming will be required, but you will find it a fairly easy job to keep your dog in a pet trim.

THE SHOW COAT

If you are planning to show your Bedlington Terrier, you will be ahead of the game if you purchase your puppy from a reputable breeder who grooms and shows her dogs. If so, this is the individual to see for grooming lessons to learn how to get your dog ready for the show ring. Grooming for the show is an art that

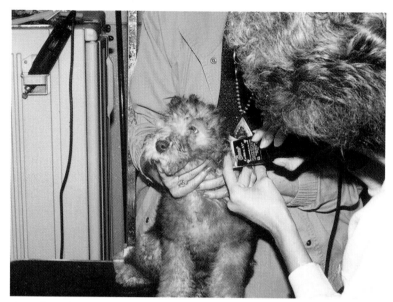

Grooming a Bedlington for the show ring can take years of practice. It is best to learn from a breeder or groomer with experience with Bedlingtons. This Serendipity pup gets his first trim.

cannot be learned in a few months. Furthermore, it is very difficult, although not impossible, to learn it from a book or from pictures.

Here are some possible scenarios for learning to groom for the show:

- You purchase your pup from a breeder who lives an easy driving distance from your home. Once a month or so, you will spend a three- or four-hour session with her learning how to trim a coat for the show ring. She will show you the art of using scissors and how to get an overall picture of a show Bedlington. She will send you home with an assignment to work on that you are to have ready when you come for your next session with your dog.

- You live in a remote area and have no help with a show coat. The best book to get is published by the BTCA and is called "Grooming and Trimming the Bedlington Terrier." Anyone may purchase this from the club. Start working on your dog, and when you attend your first shows, be sure to notice how the other dogs are trimmed.

If you are not grooming for show purposes, you do not have to be so concerned about having the topknot just so or the rear legs trimmed perfectly. Do think of the general appearance portion of the standard and try to apply this to your dog when you are grooming.

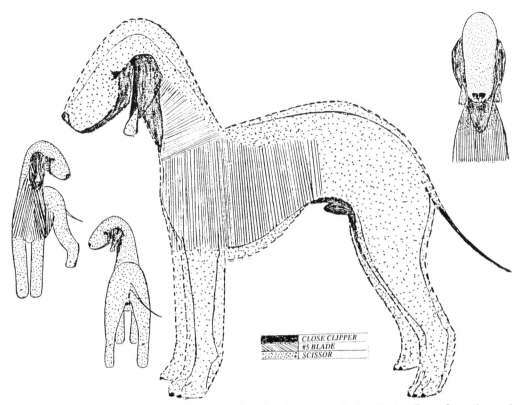

Illustrated Summary for Trimming the Bedlington Terrier. From *Grooming and Trimming the Bedlington Terrier*, published by the BTCA.

GROOMING THE PET

Pet grooming is different from grooming for the show ring because you can do much of the trimming with clippers rather than scissors. Here are the tools that you will need:

1. A grooming table—something sturdy with a rubber mat covering the top. You will need a grooming arm (or a "hangar"). You can use a table in your laundry room with an eye hook in the ceiling to hold the leash. Your dog will be comfortable even if confined, and you will be able to use both hands to work on the dog. Grooming is a very difficult and frustrating job if you try to groom without a table and a grooming arm.

2. A steel comb.

3. A slicker brush.

4. A sharp pair of barber scissors.

5. A toenail trimmer.

6. Electric clippers with a #15 (or 30 or 40) blade for close work and a #5 blade for the body.

Fuzzi Logic Agatha Cyberpup, bred by Carillon Bedlingtons, shows off her natural, untrimmed coat.

The following criteria are what the BTCA recommends for a "Utility Trim":

A quick trim for the kennel or home is possible using coarse clippers everywhere except on the legs, brisket, and head.

1. First, comb out the dog thoroughly. Then closely clip, with the finer blade, the dog's ears, face, throat, tuck-up, belly, and tail.

2. Next, with your #5 blade, start on the back of the hind legs about 3 inches above the hock joint, or where the leg begins to get thicker. Note: Cutting against the direction of hair growth gives a more even, though shorter, trim.

3. Continuing with the #5 blade, clip the front edge of the thighs, the tail root, and the whole back, but not the brisket below the widest part of the ribs. The chest and shoulders should be clipped down to the elbows. The throat and sides of the neck below the base of the ears should be clipped, leaving a strip like a horse's mane down the back of the neck, and then coming to a point just at the highest part of the shoulder blades.

4. Now, comb out the remaining hair on the legs, brisket, head, and neck. With your scissors, cut the edges of the long hair so that it blends into the clipped areas without leaving an obvious "shelf" line. Cut the hair shorter on the back of the neck, the elbows, and side of the body to the ribs into the brisket. The feet and legs should be trimmed as usual. The head, including the ears, muzzle, and topknot, should receive special attention if the dog is to look like a Bedlington.

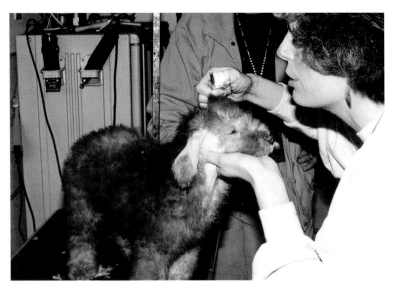

You must accustom your Bedlington to grooming procedures when he is a puppy, especially if he will be competing in the show ring.

A clipper trim is especially effective if done when the new dark coat is just beginning to come in. The areas clipped correspond exactly with the dark pattern on the ideal Bedlington.

Note that you won't learn this trim in an afternoon. But each time you trim your dog you will become more adept with the clippers and scissors. You now have a Bedlington Terrier that you can be proud of. When the two of you walk down the street, watch the attention and admiration that you will attract.

Before and after—these Serendipity pups demonstrate the difference between the trimmed and untrimmed.

If you trim regularly, it will be easier, because you can follow your set pattern. If you let the coat grow out, your previous pattern will be lost and you will have to start over again with a new pattern.

In summary, your pet should be brushed weekly and bathed as needed. Trim the toenails every month or so and plan to clip the dog every three months. Follow this plan and your dog will be clean, have a new "dress" every three months, and will look like a Bedlington Terrier—or like a lamb, as the general population says.

The Bedlington Terrier in the Show Ring

D og shows have been in existence in the US for well over 100 years. The Westminster Kennel Club dog show, held every year in New York City at the beginning of February, is the second oldest annual sporting event in the country, with only the Kentucky Derby having greater longevity. The first Westminster show was held in 1877. In 1948, Bedlington Terrier Ch. Rock Ridge Night Rocket, owned by Mr. and Mrs. William A. Rockefeller, was Best in Show at this most prestigious of canine events.

Dog shows and dog show competitions are not for everyone, but if you are intent on becoming an active breeder, you will have to be out and about at the shows, either showing your own dogs or having them shown by a professional handler.

I attended my first match show in 1964 with an Old English Sheepdog, encouraged by a friend who showed a Great Dane. Four hundred dogs were crammed into a little building. I thought that everyone was crazy, but I was intrigued. Several months later I attended my second show—the Minneapolis Kennel Club's annual all-breed show, which was benched at that time. "This," I thought, "is what a dog show is about!" Fifteen hundred dogs sitting on benches, wide aisles, breeders, and spectators exchanging stories and pedigrees. My third show was in Iowa, and I rode with a friend who had recently purchased a St. Bernard. We didn't know about dog crates, so my Sheepdog rode loose in the rear of the

Ch. Von's Bramble Buddy, the Number Three Bedlington in breed competition in 1992 and winner of 53 Bests of Breed, winning Group Fourth at the Iowa Kennel Club in 1992. Owned and handled by Paula Von Gerichten.

station wagon, my friend's wife and I sat in the midsection, and my friend drove, with the Saint sitting next to him on the front seat. The wife traveled the 300-mile trip with a whisk broom in her hand and hit the Saint on the head every time he tried to climb over the seat to go after my dog in the rear. The weather was cold and the show was held in a cow barn. This was not an easy beginning to the sport of showing dogs.

Successful showing requires dedication and preparation and should be enjoyable for both the dog and the handler.

If you are new to the show ring, attend a few local shows without your dog to see what the game is about. If you are competitive, have the time and the money to compete, and, of course, have a good dog, this may be the sport and hobby for you.

If you have not already done so, join your local all-breed club. If you are fortunate enough to live near the Chicago area or Southern California, be sure to join either one of those clubs. This is really a must for a novice to the ring. The Bedlington affiliate clubs will hold one or two seminars a year that will give you tips on how to show your dog and how to groom your dog for competition. They will have one or two match shows a year where you can practice your newly learned skills and have an opportunity to get rid of your nervousness. Match shows are run like a dog show, but they are casual and a good place for the beginner to learn. You will not receive any points toward a championship, but you will find out how a dog show is run and you will learn what will be expected of you and your dog. Entry fees at matches are minimal. This is also a good opportunity to meet the people in the breed.

Ch. Boulevardier Seltine Tiere, Number Three Bedlington, 1994, and Number Two Bedlington, 1995, in Canada; and Number Eight Bedlington, 1995, in the United States. Owned by Gail Gates and Art Perkins.

Contact your local all-breed club to find out if they offer conformation classes and start attending these classes on a regular basis. Remember, one class does not an expert make. When you think that you are ready, your dog can walk on a lead, and you feel a tiny bit of confidence, enter an AKC-licensed dog show.

Dog shows are divided into seven groups of dogs, of which the Terriers are the fourth group. The order of the groups are: Sporting, Hounds, Working, Terrier, Toys, Non-Sporting, and Herding. You will enter your dog as a Bedlington Terrier and you will enter as either a dog (male) or a bitch (female). Unless your dog is a champion, you must enter either the Puppy 6–12 Month Class, the 12–18 Month class, Novice, American-Bred (no imports), Bred by Exhibitor (if you are listed as the breeder/owner of the dog), or the Open Class. If you are inexperienced, you may want to consider the American-Bred class or the 12–18 Month Class if your dog is no longer eligible for the Puppy Class.

Marvay's Tyson, three-month-old Puppy Sweepstakes winner. Owned by Martha McVay.

The judge will place each class first, second, third, and fourth. Each class winner of the sex will compete for Winners, i.e., the best dog or bitch of the class (non-champion) dogs. After the non-champion dogs and bitches are judged, the champions of both sexes, the Winners Dog, and Winners Bitch (best of the class dogs and class bitches) will compete for Best of Breed. The judge will then select the Bedlington Terrier that he feels represents the breed the best for that day. This is the dog that will go into the Terrier Group competition representing the Bedlington.

Again, there will be four placements in the group, and the first-place Terrier will go into the Best in Show competition. There will be seven dogs in this class, one from each group. The Best in Show judge will select the dog that he feels is the best dog in the show. Thus, a dog show that started at 8:00 am with 2,000 or 3,000 dogs will finish the day with one dog that has remained undefeated and goes Best in Show.

Nine-month-old Touchstone Tyne of Marvay winning his first show at the BTCA National Specialty, Texas Kennel Club, 1987. Owned by Martha McVay.

That is basically how a dog show functions. As a newcomer to showing a dog, you will want to work toward a championship for your dog. This may take as little as three months, but more likely it will take anywhere from six months to two years, depending on how often you are able to attend shows and, of course, how often you win.

Rowland Johns wrote in 1933, "What good judges cannot resist is a dog who, having a reasonable number of good points, is able to carry himself as if he owned the whole show." The great judge Vincent Perry wrote about a particular Best in Show dog, "There is nothing wooden about her stance. She quivers with life and her eyes defy a judge to turn her down. She doesn't miss a thing going on around her. She looks and acts as if the whole thing was a delightful game which she enjoys thoroughly."

Ch. DeJeune Tobias of Marvay, finishing his championship in 1996 under breeder/judge Margaret Young Renihan and handled by owner Dess June.

Remember, participating successfully in showing dogs requires patience, perseverance, time, money, skill, and talent. It is the only sport where the amateur and the professional compete on an equal footing. The average dog-show competitor remains active for only four to five years. Personal commitments, such as children, work, and other hobbies, can be a problem to those who want to compete every weekend. More often, the competitor who does not win enough will find his interest in the sport waning. A poorly bred dog, a dog that does not like to show, and a handler who will not take the time to learn how to handle well are all deterrents to staying with the sport of dog showing. It is well to remember the advice of Holland Buckley, "If the day goes against you, your selection of shows and judges is sufficiently large to try again.

At a conformation show, Bedlington Terriers are judged on how closely they conform to the standard of the breed.

The awards are, after all, only the expression of one man's judgment, and the best of them at times overlook virtues as well as they sometimes miss bad faults."

You should contact a professional handler if you want your dog shown and are unable to do it yourself, either because of work and time commitments or because you just don't want to enter the ring and compete. A professional handler is an individual whose livelihood is handling dogs and who also often boards and grooms dogs. Be sure to inquire about the background of a handler before handing your dog over. You will want one that is familiar with the Terriers and their temperament and one who is used to working with small dogs that are put on the table for a judge to examine. You will certainly want a handler who is familiar with grooming a Bedlington. The handler should be familiar with the care and showing of a Bedlington Terrier and, above all, should be a handler who *wins*. The handler will be able to furnish one or two references if you feel that this is necessary. Be sure to inquire about all costs and find out what will be expected from you as the owner of the dog. In return, the handler will tell you what you can expect from him.

Gene McGuire showing a multiple Best in Show winning brace, Ch. D'Argo Nikolai of Bourbon and Ch. Gemar's Bourbon on the Rocks.

Through the years, there have been professional handlers who have been true friends of the Bedlington Terrier. These are individuals who have shown the great dogs and who have loved the breed. Most have been members of the BTCA and have given their time freely to help individuals within the breed. Anthony Neary was the premier Bedlington handler, piloting the great Ch. Rocket Ridge Night Rocket to spectacular wins, and was influential in bringing the Bedlington before the public eye. Joe Waterman, Robert Hutton, Robert Wendell, and David Ramsey also are prominent with their handling and grooming abilities as well as their love for the breed. In addition, Charlie Prager, Tom Gannon, and Ed Duckett all handled many Bedlingtons to their championships and to top placements, and all three later became AKC judges.

In the early years, dog showing was a sport of the wealthy who hired the professionals to handle and condition their dogs. Now, it is the usual to see the owner-handler in the ring, winning top honors with his dogs. The Bedlington Terrier has had many excellent breeder/owner/handlers who have won top honors for both their own dogs and for their clients.

I started my dog-showing days with an Old English Sheepdog. Later, I became a Scottish Terrier fancier, and later yet, a French Bulldog owner. As time went on, I became more proficient in the ring and have always maintained that it takes strength to show a

Am. Can. Ch. Carillon Boulevardier winning an Award of Merit at the Westminster Kennel Club in 1996, under breeder/judge Grace Brewin.

Ch. Carillon Bat Mercedes, with handler Kelly Hitchcock, taking Winners Bitch at the Old Dominion Kennel Club's 100th Anniversary show in 1997 under breeder/judge Anna Katona.

large breed and intelligence to show a small one. I also learned that you can start your show career not having an inkling of what you are to do and, through time and practice, you can become quite accomplished.

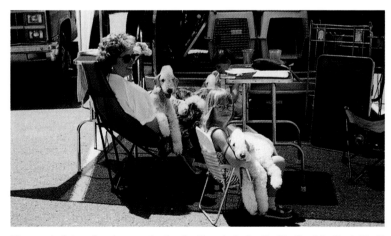

The sport of dog showing can be fun for the whole family. Dr. Cynthia Cook Pruitt and her daughters relax after the ring.

BEDLINGTON TERRIER NATIONAL AND SPECIALTY WINNERS 1982–1998

1982

BTCA 50ᵀᴴ ANNIVERSARY • ELIZABETH, NJ

BEST OF BREED
Ch. Willow Wind Flirtation, Owner: David Ramsey

BEST OF WINNERS/WINNERS DOG
Westlands Blue Star, Owner: R. S. Hatifield

BEST OF OPPOSITE SEX
Ch. Barma Olympia Bonny Brae, Owners: Frank Majocha and Joan Stackhouse

WINNERS BITCH
OK's Lady Diana of Valgo, Owners: James and Marilyn O'Keefe

REGIONAL SPECIALTY • BEDLINGTON TERRIER CLUB OF GREATER CHICAGO

BEST OF BREED
Flurry's Rusty Jones, Owner: Dolores Schmidt

BEST OF WINNERS/WINNERS DOG
Tiffanie's Riverboat Blues, Owners: Darlene and John Ready

BEST OF OPPOSITE SEX
Ch. Lochmist Cotton Candy, Owner: Dolores Jean Jackson

WINNERS BITCH
Lochmist Dulciana, Owner: Mrs. Thomas J. Mahoney

REGIONAL SPECIALTY • THE BEDLINGTON TERRIER CLUB OF THE WEST

BEST OF BREED
Ch. Vu-Pointe's Bianca, Owners: Barbara and Douglas Swigart and Duane Rozema

BEST OF WINNERS/WINNERS DOG
Bentley's Smokey Bear, Owner: Thomas H. Trainer, Jr.

BEST OF OPPOSITE SEX
Ch. Gemar Blue Boy of Renaissance, Owner: Sheila Wallace

WINNERS BITCH
PIMA Sunshine of Vah-Ki, Owner: Bertha Parkhurst

NATIONAL SPECIALTY • MONTGOMERY COUNTY

BEST OF BREED
Ch. Lucinda's Tim of Gold Grove, Owner: Sharon Pflueger

BEST OF WINNERS/WINNERS DOG
Tiffanie's Tickle Your Butsky, Owners: John S. and Darlene Ready

BEST OF OPPOSITE SEX
Ch. Willow Wind Flirtation, Owner: David P. Ramsey

WINNERS BITCH
Berkshire's Bachelor Button, Owner: Loretta Moffatt

BEDLINGTON TERRIER NATIONAL AND SPECIALTY WINNERS 1982–1998

1983

BTCA SPECIALTY SHOW • ELIZABETH, NJ

BEST OF BREED
Ch. Vu-Pointe's Bianca, Owners: Barbara and Douglas Swigart

BEST OF WINNERS/WINNERS BITCH
Siwash Blue Keeley, Owners: Don and Shirley Martin

BEST OF OPPOSITE SEX
Ch. Merwyn Prescott Quiger, Owner: Mary Squires

WINNERS DOG
Starcastle's Free Spirit, Owners: Michael and Joanne Relly and Nancy Rappaport

REGIONAL SPECIALTY • BEDLINGTON TERRIER CLUB OF GREATER CHICAGO

BEST OF BREED
Ch. Lucinda's Tim of Gold Grove, Owner: Sharon Pflueger

BEST OF WINNERS/WINNERS DOG
Celin's Hopi's Kachina Fire God, Owner: Jean Mathieu

BEST OF OPPOSITE SEX
Ch. Willow Wind Social Butterfly, Owner: David Ramsey

WINNERS BITCH
Noel's Tia Gemar, Owner: Gene Mc Guire

REGIONAL SPECIALTY • THE BEDLINGTON TERRIER CLUB OF THE WEST

BEST OF BREED
Ch. Sir Lancelot of Milam St., Owner: Mrs. Elizabeth Williams

BEST OF WINNERS/WINNERS BITCH
Lady Mercedes of Torrey Pines, Owner: Lisa De Malvoi

BEST OF OPPOSITE SEX
Ch. Lady Bentley of Cromwell, Owner: Thomas H. Trainer, Jr.

WINNERS DOG
Monte the Silver Streak, Owner: Barbara Kramer Lee

NATIONAL SPECIALTY • MONTGOMERY COUNTY

BEST OF BREED
Ch. Merwyn Prescott Quiger, Owner: Mary R. Squires

BEST OF WINNERS/WINNERS DOG
Sir Winston of Nissequogue, Owner: Patricia Briglia

BEST OF OPPOSITE SEX
Ch. Willow Wind Social Butterfly, Owner: David Ramsey

WINNERS BITCH
Tiffanie Christmas Star, Owners: Bette and Gary Rotert

BEDLINGTON TERRIER NATIONAL AND SPECIALTY WINNERS 1982–1998

1984

BTCA SPECIALTY SHOW • ELIZABETH, NJ

BEST OF BREED
Ch. Vansan's Crystal Singer, Owners: L. Goldsmith and E. Miner

BEST OF WINNERS/WINNERS DOG
Berkshire's Special K, Owner: Loretta Moffatt

BEST OF OPPOSITE SEX
Ch. Sir Lancelot of Milam St., Owner: Elizabeth Williams

WINNERS BITCH
Marten's Bluebonnet O'Bourbon, Owners: Coral and Allan Anderson and Roger Widener

REGIONAL SPECIALTY • BEDLINGTON TERRIER CLUB OF GREATER CHICAGO

BEST OF BREED
Ch. Siwash Blue Keeley, Owners: Don and Shirley Martin

BEST OF WINNERS/WINNERS DOG
Whirlwynd's Country Bumpkin, Owner: Beth Hollandsworth

BEST OF OPPOSITE SEX
Ch. Claremont Anchor Man, Owners: Lucy Heyman and Rosemarie Ingate

WINNERS BITCH
Nosehill Amethyst of Siwash, Owners: Don and Shirley Martin

REGIONAL SPECIALTY • THE BEDLINGTON TERRIER CLUB OF THE WEST

BEST OF BREED
Ch. Tiffanie's Tickle Your Butsky, Owners: Bee Spencer and Darlene Ready

BEST OF WINNERS/WINNERS BITCH
Vu-Point's-Cromwell's Niki, Owner: Sandy Miller

BEST OF OPPOSITE SEX
Ch. Vansan's Crystal Singer, Owners: Lucretia G. Goldsmith and Earl C. Mines

WINNERS DOG
Lucinda's Blew Ashley, Owner: Claudia Raszka

NATIONAL SPECIALTY • MONTGOMERY COUNTY

BEST OF BREED/BEST OF WINNERS/WINNERS DOG
Lochmist Blue Stuff of Billiken, Owner: Virginia H. Luft

BEST OF OPPOSITE SEX
Ch. Iverness Daphne, Owners: James W. and Helen H. Heintz

BEDLINGTON TERRIER NATIONAL AND SPECIALTY WINNERS 1982–1998

1985

NATIONAL ROTATING SPECIALTY • HOUSTON KENNEL CLUB

BEST OF BREED
Dejeune Witch of the Wood, Owner: Dess June

BEST OF WINNERS/WINNERS DOG
Wedgewood Montgomery, Owners: Robert Tuohy and Mary Kupcho

BEST OF OPPOSITE SEX
Ch. Lucinda's Blew Ashley, Owner: Claudia Raszka

WINNERS BITCH
Willow Wind Infatuation, Owner: Kay Jeffers

REGIONAL SPECIALTY • BEDLINGTON TERRIER CLUB OF GREATER CHICAGO

BEST OF BREED
Ch. Willow Wind Centurian, Owner: David Ramsey

BEST OF WINNERS/WINNERS DOG
Wedgewood Montgomery, Owners: Robert Tuohy and Mary Kupcho

BEST OF OPPOSITE SEX
Ch. Cleo's Ivy Halo, Owner: Beverly Brooks

WINNERS BITCH
Jinji Di Shepsel, Owners: Miryam and Morris Rubenstein

REGIONAL SPECIALTY • THE BEDLINGTON TERRIER CLUB OF THE WEST

BEST OF BREED
Ch. Lucinda's Blew Ashley, Owner: Claudia Raszka

BEST OF WINNERS/WINNERS BITCH
Lady Bentley's Heather Frost, Owner: Terry Olson

BEST OF OPPOSITE SEX
Ch. VuPointe's Quest For Best, Owners: Barbara and Douglas Swigart

WINNERS DOG
Lucinda's High Noon Cooper, Owners: Martin and Josephine Sykes

NATIONAL SPECIALTY • MONTGOMERY COUNTY

BEST OF BREED
Ch. Willow Wind Centurian, Owner: David Ramsey

BEST OF WINNERS/WINNERS DOG
Highpoint's Regal Carriage, Owners: James and Elaine Haskett

BEST OF OPPOSITE SEX
Ch. Dejeune Witch of the Wood, Owner: Dess June

WINNERS BITCH
Willow Wind Capucine Cherie, Owner: Marcel Rancourt

BEDLINGTON TERRIER NATIONAL AND SPECIALTY WINNERS 1982–1998

1986

NATIONAL ROTATING SPECIALTY • LOUISVILLE, KY

BEST OF BREED
Ch. Willow Wind Centurian, Owner: David Ramsey

BEST OF WINNERS/WINNERS DOG
Sandon's Oakhill Will O'Wisp, Owners: Sandra Miles and Foley Harper

BEST OF OPPOSITE SEX
Ch. Dejeune Witch of the Wood, Owner: Dess June

WINNERS BITCH
Lady Abbey of Amherst, Owner: Patricia Sofranko

REGIONAL SPECIALTY • BEDLINGTON TERRIER CLUB OF GREATER CHICAGO

BEST OF BREED
Ch. Marten's Graham Cracker Jr., Owners: Lyle and Darlene Martens

BEST OF WINNERS/WINNERS BITCH
Gemar's Summer Cloud, Owner: Susan Mendenhall

BEST OF OPPOSITE SEX
Ch. Oakhill 'n Sandon Carnelian, Owners: Sandy Miles and Foley Harper

WINNERS DOG
Gemar's Gabriel, Owners: Gene McGuire and G. Ochsenschlager

NATIONAL SPECIALTY • MONTGOMERY COUNTY

BEST OF BREED
Ch. Willow Wind Centurian, Owners: David P. Ramsey and Allen M. Sheimo

BEST OF WINNERS/WINNERS DOG
Sandon Oakhill Halley's Comet, Owners: Sandra Miles and Foley Harper

BEST OF OPPOSITE SEX
Ch. Willow Wind Blue Emerald, Owners: David P. Ramsey and R. W. and A. M. Hubbard

WINNERS BITCH
Thika of Rowanoaks, Owners: Constance M. Willemsen and Rowanoaks Kennels (Reg)

BEDLINGTON TERRIER NATIONAL AND SPECIALTY WINNERS 1982–1998

1987

NATIONAL ROTATING SPECIALTY • DALLAS KENNEL CLUB

BEST OF BREED
Ch. Willow Wind Centurian, Owners: David P. Ramsey and Allen M. Sheimo

BEST OF WINNERS/ BEST OF OPPOSITE SEX/WINNERS BITCH
Willow Wind Pardon Me Boys, Owner: David Ramsey

WINNERS DOG
Touchstone Tyne of Marvay, Owner: Martha McVay

REGIONAL SPECIALTY • BEDLINGTON TERRIER CLUB OF GREATER CHICAGO

BEST OF BREED
Ch. Willow Wind Centurian, Owners: David P. Ramsey and Allen M. Sheimo

BEST OF WINNERS/WINNERS DOG
Sayles Be Still My Heart, Owners: Thomas and Kristin Hamernik

BEST OF OPPOSITE SEX
Gemar's Morning Dove, Owners: Gretchen Ochsenschlager and Gene McGuire

WINNERS BITCH
Morning Star of Dejeune, Owner: Dess June

REGIONAL SPECIALTY • THE BEDLINGTON TERRIER CLUB OF THE WEST

BEST OF BREED
Ch. Bentley's Smokey Bear, Owner: Thomas Trainer

BEST OF WINNERS/WINNERS DOG
Rampion of Rowanoaks, Owner: Constance Willemsen

BEST OF OPPOSITE SEX/WINNERS BITCH
Marvay's Qsilver Puff O'Smoke, Owner: Judy Smith

NATIONAL SPECIALTY • MONTGOMERY COUNTY

BEST OF BREED
Ch. Willow Wind Centurian, Owners: David P. Ramsey and Allen M. Sheimo

BEST OF WINNERS/WINNERS DOG
Barma Sentinel of Willow Wind, Owners: David Ramsey and Frank Majocha

BEST OF OPPOSITE SEX
Ch. Willow Wind Pardon Me Boys, Owners: Maggie Rodenbach and David Ramsey

WINNERS BITCH
Bourbon-Victoria Rising Star, Owner: Douglas Lehr

BEDLINGTON TERRIER NATIONAL AND SPECIALTY WINNERS 1982–1998

1988

NATIONAL ROTATING SPECIALTY • ST. PETERSBURG, FL

BEST OF BREED
Ch. Barma's Rudi of Riegel Road, Owners: Carrol Wermes and Frank Majocha

BEST OF WINNERS/WINNERS BITCH
Elkwood Devine Ms. Emma, Owners: Steve Dunn and John Roark

BEST OF OPPOSITE SEX
Ch. Willow Wind Pardon Me Boys, Owners: Maggie Rodenbach and David Ramsey

WINNERS DOG
Elkwood's Windy Done Justice, Owner: Karen Goula

REGIONAL SPECIALTY • BEDLINGTON TERRIER CLUB OF GREATER CHICAGO

BEST OF BREED
Ch. Serendipity Salieri, Owner: Lucy Heyman

BEST OF WINNERS/WINNERS BITCH
Xerxes Candied Violet of Cleo, Owner: Florence Brown

BEST OF OPPOSITE SEX
Ch. Vanole's Victoria, Owner: Ralph Hogancamp

WINNERS DOG
Carillon Platinum to Th'Core, Owners: Kay Audra Jeffers and Lucy Heyman

REGIONAL SPECIALTY • THE BEDLINGTON TERRIER CLUB OF THE WEST

BEST OF BREED
Ch. Willow Wind Centurian, Owners: David P. Ramsey and Allen M. Sheimo

BEST OF WINNERS/WINNERS BITCH/BEST OF OPPOSITE SEX
Liebchen Von Cromwell, Owners: Sandy Miller and Duane Rozema

WINNERS DOG
Bentley Ben Cromwell, Owner: Kharlene Boxenbaum

NATIONAL SPECIALTY • MONTGOMERY COUNTY

BEST OF BREED
Ch. Willow Wind Centurian, Owners: David P. Ramsey and Allen M. Sheimo

BEST OF WINNERS/WINNERS BITCH
Siwash Lady Luck, Owners: Don and Shirley Martin

BEST OF OPPOSITE SEX
Ch. Willow Wind Pardon Me Boys, Owners: Maggie Rodenbach and David Ramsey

WINNERS DOG
Saralynn's Azure Orbit, Owner: Margaret Dunlop

BEDLINGTON TERRIER NATIONAL AND SPECIALTY WINNERS 1982–1998

1989

NATIONAL ROTATING SPECIALTY • TRENTON, NJ

BEST OF BREED
Ch. Willow Wind Centurian, Owners: David P. Ramsey and Allen M. Sheimo

BEST OF WINNERS/WINNERS DOG
Liberty's Sentimental Journey, Owner: Douglas Lehr

BEST OF OPPOSITE SEX
Ch. Willow Wind Indigo Sprite, Owner: Kathy Donovan

WINNERS BITCH
Chelsea's Love is Blue, Owner: Linda Miller

REGIONAL SPECIALTY • BEDLINGTON TERRIER CLUB OF GREATER CHICAGO

BEST OF BREED
Ch. Willow Wind Centurian, Owners: David P. Ramsey and Allen M. Sheimo

BEST OF WINNERS/WINNERS BITCH
Willow Wind Corniche, Owners: Mark Maryanski and David Ramsey

BEST OF OPPOSITE SEX
Ch. Siwash Lady Luck, Owners: Don and Shirley Martin

WINNERS DOG
Dynasty's Against All Odds, Owner: Penny Harlan

REGIONAL SPECIALTY • THE BEDLINGTON TERRIER CLUB OF THE WEST

BEST OF BREED
Ch. Willow Wind Centurian, Owners: David P. Ramsey and Allen M. Sheimo

BEST OF WINNERS/WINNERS DOG
Marvay's Taylor Made, Owner: Martha McVay

BEST OF OPPOSITE SEX
Ch. Marvay's QSilver Puff O'Smoke, Owner: Judy Smith

WINNERS BITCH
Willow Wind Bonnie Miss T, Owner: Fay Johnson, M.D.

NATIONAL SPECIALTY • MONTGOMERY COUNTY

BEST OF BREED/BEST OF WINNERS/WINNERS DOG
Willow Wind Silver Wraith, Owner: Mark Maryanski

BEST OF OPPOSITE SEX/WINNERS BITCH
Meadowsweet O Doutelle, Owner: Vanessa Sypher

BEDLINGTON TERRIER NATIONAL AND SPECIALTY WINNERS 1982–1998

1990

NATIONAL ROTATING SPECIALTY • LOUISVILLE, KY

BEST OF BREED
Ch. Willow Wind Centurian, Owners: David P. Ramsey and Allen M. Sheimo

BEST OF WINNERS/WINNERS BITCH/BEST OF OPPOSITE SEX
Sakura's Dream Desire, Owner: Vicki Schawo

WINNERS DOG
W-W Cynosure of BRBN, Owners: Thomas Walter and Roger Widener

REGIONAL SPECIALTY • BEDLINGTON TERRIER CLUB OF GREATER CHICAGO

BEST OF BREED
Ch. Willow Wind Centurian, Owners: David P. Ramsey and Allen M. Sheimo

BEST OF WINNERS/WINNERS BITCH
Alchris-Inverness Cecily, Owners: Helen and James Heintz

BEST OF OPPOSITE SEX
Ch. Tante Mimi Di Shepsel, Owners: Morris and Miryam Rubenstein

WINNERS DOG
W-W Sport Section of Bourbon, Owners: Michael and Joanne Stadther

REGIONAL SPECIALTY • THE BEDLINGTON TERRIER CLUB OF THE WEST

BEST OF BREED
Ch. Willow Wind Centurian, Owners: David P. Ramsey and Allen M. Sheimo

BEST OF WINNERS/WINNERS DOG
Tiffanie's Sir Smedley, Owner: Mary Goodhue

BEST OF OPPOSITE SEX
Ch. Sara's Tickle Your Toes, Owners: Sara Fury Osmonson and Darlene Ready

WINNERS BITCH
Willow Wind Tassie Miss T, Owners: Fay Johnson, M.D. and David Ramsey

NATIONAL SPECIALTY • MONTGOMERY COUNTY

BEST OF BREED
Ch. Sweetbriar's Carillon Cody, Owners: Debora Regan and Lucy Heyman

BEST OF WINNERS/WINNERS BITCH
Chelsea's Merlyn of Blue Nob, Owners: Jean and Jeff Stark

BEST OF OPPOSITE SEX
Ch. Siwash Blue Keeley, Owners: Shirley and Don Martin

WINNERS DOG
Willow Wind Takin' It Easy, Owner: Janice Bedient

BEDLINGTON TERRIER NATIONAL AND SPECIALTY WINNERS 1982–1998

1991

NATIONAL ROTATING SPECIALTY • GWTF SILVER ANNIVERSARY

BEST OF BREED
Ch. Carillon Platinum to Th'Core, Owner: Kharlene Boxenbaum

BEST OF WINNERS/WINNERS BITCH
Sara's Tickle Softly, Owner: Sara Fury Osmonson

BEST OF OPPOSITE SEX
Ch. Cleo's Wind in the Willow, Owners: Beverly Brooks and David Ramsey

WINNERS DOG
Chelsea's Stolen Heart Blues, Owners: Linda Miller and Sandra Martin

REGIONAL SPECIALTY • BEDLINGTON TERRIER CLUB OF GREATER CHICAGO

BEST OF BREED
Ch. Cleo's Wind in the Willow, Owners: Beverly Brooks and David Ramsey

BEST OF WINNERS/WINNERS BITCH
Pawzhenton's Liberty Belle, Owners: Chris Johnson and Lisa Bettis

BEST OF OPPOSITE SEX
Ch. Barma's Rudi of Riegel Road, Owners: Carrol Wermes and Frank Majocha

WINNERS DOG
Willow Wind Takin' It Easy, Owner: Janice Bedient

REGIONAL SPECIALTY • THE BEDLINGTON TERRIER CLUB OF THE WEST

BEST OF BREED
Ch. Cleo's Wind in the Willow, Owners: Beverly Brooks and David Ramsey

BEST OF WINNERS/WINNERS DOG
Lucinda's Lucky Gulliver, Owner: Garrison Singer

BEST OF OPPOSITE SEX
Ch. Tiffanie's Brass Monkey, Owner: Chris Williams

WINNERS BITCH
Briargrove's Who's That Girl, Owners: Beverly Brandes and Judy Matusek

NATIONAL SPECIALTY • MONTGOMERY COUNTY

BEST OF BREED
Ch. Cleo's Wind in the Willow, Owners: David Ramsey and Carol and Herb Slattery, Jr.

BEST OF WINNERS/WINNERS BITCH
Meadowsweet KT O'Berkshire, Owner: Loretta Moffatt

BEST OF OPPOSITE SEX
Ch. Willow Wind Play It My Way, Owner: Maggie Maier

WINNERS DOG
Sudor's British Sterling, Owners: Kenneth Russell and Dolores King

BEDLINGTON TERRIER NATIONAL AND SPECIALTY WINNERS 1982–1998

1992

NATIONAL ROTATING SPECIALTY • LOUISVILLE, KY

BEST OF BREED
Ch. Willow Wind Play It My Way, Owner: David Ramsey

BEST OF WINNERS/WINNERS BITCH
Sweetbriar's Clover Carillon, Owners: Deborah and Patrick Regan

BEST OF OPPOSITE SEX
Ch. Inverness Deirdre, Owners: James and Helen Heintz

WINNERS DOG
Victoria-Darbyshire Bentley, Owner: Candace Andelman

REGIONAL SPECIALTY • BEDLINGTON TERRIER CLUB OF GREATER CHICAGO

BEST OF BREED
Ch. Barma's Rudi of Riegel Road, Owners: Frank Majocha and Carrol Wermes

BEST OF WINNERS/WINNERS
Barma's Wee Willie Wyncote (Owner not listed)

BEST OF OPPOSITE SEX
Sweetbriar's Clover Carillon, Owners: Deborah and Patrick Regan

WINNERS BITCH
Barma's Lady Jane Grey, Owner: Paula Von Gerichten

REGIONAL SPECIALTY • THE BEDLINGTON TERRIER CLUB OF THE WEST

BEST OF BREED
Ch. Tiffanie's Sir Smedley, Owner: Mary Goodhue

BEST OF WINNERS/WINNERS
Ch. Sara's Tickle the Ivories, Owner: Margaret Dunlop

BEST OF OPPOSITE SEX
Ch. Sara's Tickle Your Toes, Owners: Sara Osmonson and Margaret Dunlop

NATIONAL SPECIALTY • MONTGOMERY COUNTY

BEST OF BREED
Ch. Willow Wind Play It My Way, Owner: David Ramsey

BEST OF WINNERS/BEST OF OPPOSITE SEX /WINNERS BITCH
Bistry's Daydream Believer, Owner: Carole Ann Diehl

WINNERS DOG
Graystone Gift of Magic, Owners: Richard and Rosemarie Anderson

BEDLINGTON TERRIER NATIONAL AND SPECIALTY WINNERS 1982–1998

1993

NATIONAL ROTATING SPECIALTY • HOUSTON KENNEL CLUB

BEST OF BREED/BEST OF WINNERS/WINNERS BITCH
NXS Maggie-T-Anne, Owners: Robert and Barbara Tuohy

BEST OF OPPOSITE SEX
Ch. Liberty's Rain Beau Bleu, Owners: Doug Lehr and Desiree Williams

WINNERS DOG
Willow Wind Heir Apparent, Owners: Kay Audra Tarnopol and David Ramsey

REGIONAL SPECIALTY • BEDLINGTON TERRIER CLUB OF GREATER CHICAGO

BEST OF BREED
Ch. Willow Wind Play It My Way, Owner: David Ramsey

BEST OF WINNERS/WINNERS DOG
Ch. Liberty's Rain Beau Bleu, Owners: Doug Lehr and Desiree Williams

BEST OF OPPOSITE SEX/WINNERS BITCH
Willow Wind Blue Jeans, Owner: Lucy Jane Myers

REGIONAL SPECIALTY • THE BEDLINGTON TERRIER CLUB OF THE WEST

BEST OF BREED
Ch. Tiffanie's Sir Smedley, Owner: Mary Goodhue

BEST OF WINNERS/WINNERS DOG
Sara's Tickle the Ivories, Owner: Margaret Dunlop

BEST OF OPPOSITE SEX
Ch. Sara's Tickle Your Toes, Owners: Sara Fury Osmonson and Margaret Dunlop

WINNERS BITCH
Tyneside X'mas Star, Owner: Don Smiley

NATIONAL SPECIALTY • MONTGOMERY COUNTY

BEST OF BREED
Ch. Liberty's Rain Beau Bleu, Owners: Doug Lehr and Desiree Williams

BEST OF WINNERS/WINNERS DOG
Lucinda's Little Pistol, Owners: B. Robertson, C. Raszka, and M. Maxwell Pendi

BEST OF OPPOSITE SEX
Ch. Sudor's White Linen, Owners: Kelli Hitchcock and Dolores King

WINNERS BITCH
Carillon No Sudor, Owner: Dolores King

BEDLINGTON TERRIER NATIONAL AND SPECIALTY WINNERS 1982–1998

1994

NATIONAL ROTATING SPECIALTY • ST. PETERSBURG, FL

BEST OF BREED
Ch. Oakhill N Sandon Fiesta Flirt, Owners: Foley Harper and Sandra Miles

BEST OF WINNERS/WINNERS DOG
NXS My Blue Heaven, Owner: Beverly Brandes

BEST OF OPPOSITE SEX
Ch. NXS Raynman, Owner: Beverly Brandes

WINNERS BITCH
Touchwood Nimbus, Owners: Jean and Richard Bolt

REGIONAL SPECIALTY • BEDLINGTON TERRIER CLUB OF GREATER CHICAGO

BEST OF BREED
Ch. Willow Wind Play It My Way, Owner: David Ramsey

BEST OF WINNERS/WINNERS DOG
Touchwood Raffles, Owner: Lynn Hall

BEST OF OPPOSITE SEX/WINNERS BITCH
Willow Wind Mustang Sally, Owner: David Ramsey

REGIONAL SPECIALTY • THE BEDLINGTON TERRIER CLUB OF THE WEST

BEST OF BREED
Ch. NXS Raynman, Owner: Beverly Brandes

BEST OF WINNERS/WINNERS DOG
Valgo's Rae of NXS, Owners: Robin Boyette and Meri Coggins

BEST OF OPPOSITE SEX/WINNERS BITCH
Silvery Moon Rainey's Ladyblu, Owner: Terri Cardoni

NATIONAL SPECIALTY • MONTGOMERY COUNTY

BEST OF BREED
Ch. Sudor's White Linen, Owners: Kelli and Jeff Hitchcock

BEST OF WINNERS/WINNERS DOG
Kel-Ti's Maximum Overdrive, Owners: Kelli and Jeff Hitchcock and Tina Humphries

BEST OF OPPOSITE SEX
Ch. Willow Wind Family Jewels, Owners: Frank Majocha and David Ramsey

WINNERS BITCH
Victoria-Bch Baby Mini Pearl, Owner: Coral Anderson

BEDLINGTON TERRIER NATIONAL AND SPECIALTY WINNERS 1982–1998

1995

NATIONAL ROTATING SPECIALTY • LOUISVILLE, KY

BEST OF BREED
Ch. Silvery Moon Rainey's Ladyblu, Owner: Terri Cardoni

BEST OF WINNERS/WINNERS BITCH
Touchwood's Sheer Bliss, Owners: Donna Jenkins and Linda Cain

BEST OF OPPOSITE SEX
Ch. Willow Wind Family Jewels, Owners: Frank Majocha and David Ramsey

WINNERS DOG
Willow Wind Money Talks, Owner: David Ramsey

REGIONAL SPECIALTY • BEDLINGTON TERRIER CLUB OF GREATER CHICAGO

BEST OF BREED
Ch. Willow Wind Money Talks, Owners: David Ramsey and Kerry Himmelberger

BEST OF WINNERS/BEST OF OPPOSITE SEX /WINNERS BITCH
Seabreeze of Tamarack, Owner: Sally De Kold

WINNERS DOG
Tawny Blue's Angel's Dues, Owner: Deborah Kmiecik

REGIONAL SPECIALTY • THE BEDLINGTON TERRIER CLUB OF THE WEST

BEST OF BREED
Ch. Silvery Moon Rainey's Ladyblu, Owners: Terri Cardoni and Beverly Brandes

BEST OF WINNERS/WINNERS DOG
NXS Raynbow, Owner: Beverly Brandes

BEST OF OPPOSITE SEX
Ch. Willow Wind Money Talks, Owners: David Ramsey and Kerry Himmelberger

WINNERS BITCH
Valgo's Whisper in the Wind, Owners: Tammy and Richard Vranich

NATIONAL ROTATING SPECIALTY • GREAT WESTERN

BEST OF BREED
Ch. Willow Wind Money Talks, Owners: David Ramsey and Kerry Himmelberger

BEST OF WINNERS/WINNERS DOG
NXS Raynbow, Owner: Beverly Brandes

BEST OF OPPOSITE SEX
Ch. Silvery Moon Rainey's Ladyblu, Owners: Terri Cardoni and Beverly Brandes

WINNERS BITCH
Valgo's Lacey, Owners: Marjorie Hanson and Dee Holm

NATIONAL SPECIALTY • MONTGOMERY COUNTY

BEST OF BREED
Ch. Willow Wind Money Talks, Owners: David Ramsey and Kerry Himmelberger

BEST OF WINNERS/WINNERS DOG
NXS XXX's & OOO's, Owner: Beverly Brandes

BEST OF OPPOSITE SEX
Ch. Willow Wind Simple Dream, Owner: David Ramsey

WINNERS BITCH
Touchwood's Sheer Bliss, Owners: Donna Jenkins and Linda Cain

BEDLINGTON TERRIER NATIONAL AND SPECIALTY WINNERS 1982–1998

1996

NATIONAL ROTATING SPECIALTY • MINNEAPOLIS, MN

BEST OF BREED/BEST OF WINNERS/WINNERS DOG
Gemar's Anything Goes, Owners: Gene McGuire and Gretchen Ochs

BEST OF OPPOSITE SEX
Ch. Nimbleby Rapartee, Owner: David Tollefsen

WINNERS BITCH
Barnsnap Barmy Breezes, Owner: Tina Westphal

REGIONAL SPECIALTY • BEDLINGTON TERRIER CLUB OF GREATER CHICAGO

BEST OF BREED
Ch. Willow Wind Money Talks, Owners: David Ramsey and Kerry Himmelberger

BEST OF WINNERS/WINNERS BITCH
Sayles Two Heart Harmony, Owners: Thomas and Kristin Hammernik

BEST OF OPPOSITE SEX
Ch. Willow Wind It's My Party, Owners: Jacquelyn Fogel and David Ramsey

WINNERS DOG
EJ's Irish Bramble Bryar, Owner: Paula Von Gerichten

REGIONAL SPECIALTY • THE BEDLINGTON TERRIER CLUB OF THE WEST

BEST OF BREED
Ch. Valgo's Rae of NXS, Owners: Robin Boyette and Marjorie Hanson

BEST OF WINNERS/WINNERS DOG
Valgo's Stargazer, Owner: Marjorie Hanson

BEST OF OPPOSITE SEX/WINNERS BITCH
Black Sheep's Duckling Sudor, Owners: Mr. and Mrs. George Beveridge

NATIONAL SPECIALTY • MONTGOMERY COUNTY

BEST OF BREED
Ch. Willow Wind Money Talks, Owners: David Ramsey and Kerry Himmelberger

BEST OF WINNERS/WINNERS DOG
Bonnybrook's Magical Sudor, Owners: Dolores King and Kristen Dorsey

BEST OF OPPOSITE SEX
Ch. Willow Wind Pardon Me Boys, Owner: Maggie Maier

WINNERS BITCH
Sudor's Magic Noir, Owners: Kristen Dorsey and Dolores King

BEDLINGTON TERRIER NATIONAL AND SPECIALTY WINNERS1982–1998

1997

NATIONAL ROTATING SPECIALTY • PERRY, GA

BEST OF BREED/BEST OF WINNERS/WINNERS DOG
Sandon N' Oakhill Wholly Smoke, Owners: Sandra Miles and Foley Harper

BEST OF OPPOSITE SEX
Sandon N' Oakhill Cheyna Star, Owners: Sandra Miles and Foley Harper

WINNERS BITCH
Devonshire Quick As A Wink, Owner: Harriett Whitbread

REGIONAL SPECIALTY • BEDLINGTON TERRIER CLUB OF GREATER CHICAGO

BEST OF BREED
Ch. Willow Wind It's My Party, Owners: Jacquelyn Fogel and David Ramsey

BEST OF WINNERS/WINNERS BITCH
Kel-Ti Sweetbriar's Game Miss Conduct, Owners: Tracey Pollok and Deborah Regan

BEST OF OPPOSITE SEX
Ch. Lord Derby of Chimneyhouse, Owners: Fred and Sally Schill

WINNERS DOG
Sayles Windwalker, Owners: Thomas and Kirstin Lou Kloet-Hammernik

REGIONAL SPECIALTY • THE BEDLINGTON TERRIER CLUB OF THE WEST

BEST OF BREED
Ch. Willow Wind Vanity Fair, Owners: Nancy and Sang Bong Han

BEST OF WINNERS/WINNERS DOG
Wildwynd's Blue Skyes, Owners: Tammy and Richard Vranich

BEST OF OPPOSITE SEX
Ch. Valgo's Rockin Rae, Owners: Robin Boyette, Marjorie Hanson, and Christel Murdock

WINNERS BITCH
Valgo's Lacey, Owners: Marjorie Hanson and Dee Holm

NATIONAL SPECIALTY • MONTGOMERY COUNTY

BEST OF BREED
Ch. Sir Robert, Owner: Robert J. Andras

BEST OF WINNERS/WINNERS DOG
Oakhill Sandon Just in Time, Owners: Foley Harper and Sandra Miles

BEST OF OPPOSITE SEX
Ch. Kel-Ti's Sudor She's No Angel, Owners: Kelli Hitchcock, Tina Humphries, and Dolores King

WINNERS BITCH
DanKen's Madeira, Owners: Ken Russell and Dan Holliday

BEDLINGTON TERRIER NATIONAL AND SPECIALTY WINNERS 1982–1998

1998

NATIONAL ROTATING SPECIALTY • COLUMBIA TERRIER ASSOCIATION OF MARYLAND

BEST OF BREED
Ch. Willow Wind Aggravation, Owners: Carole Diehl and Rosemary Anderson

BEST OF WINNERS/WINNERS BITCH
Good Gollie Miss Mollie, Owner: Donna Reddicento

BEST OF OPPOSITE SEX
Sandon N' Oakhill Bold Baron, Owners: Sandra Miles and Foley Harper

WINNERS DOG
Liberty's Rain Beau Connection, Owners: Doug Lehr, Desiree Williams, and Beverly Brooks

REGIONAL SPECIALTY • BEDLINGTON TERRIER CLUB OF GREATER CHICAGO

BEST OF BREED
Ch. Willow Wind It's My Party, Owner: Jacquelyn Fogel

BEST OF WINNERS/WINNERS DOG
Willow Wind Tenure, Owners: Nancy and Sang Bong Han

BEST OF OPPOSITE SEX
Ch. First Class Two Tone Joe Tamarack, Owner: Jacquelyn Fogel

WINNERS BITCH
Gemar Tyk's Fantasia, Owner: Karen Yohnka

REGIONAL SPECIALTY • THE BEDLINGTON TERRIER CLUB OF THE WEST

BEST OF BREED
Ch. Willow Wind Tenure, Owners: Nancy and Sang Bong Han

BEST OF WINNERS/WINNERS BITCH
NXS Last Dance, Owner: Beverly Brandes

BEST OF OPPOSITE SEX
Ch. Chelsea's Blue Cameo, Owner: Mary Joe Dunn

WINNERS DOG
Carillon Fuzzi Logic Cyrix, Owner: Annette Gustavson

NATIONAL SPECIALTY • MONTGOMERY COUNTY

BEST OF BREED
Ch. Silvery Moon Unforgettable, Owners: Kay and Richard Kraft

BEST OF WINNERS/WINNERS BITCH
Meadowsweet Summer's Hot, Owner: Vanessa Sypher

BEST OF OPPOSITE SEX
Ch. Willow Wind Tenure, Owners: Nancy and Sang Bong Han

WINNERS DOG
Lambert's Donnegal Piper, Owner: Not listed by AKC

Gallery of Winning Bedlington Terriers

Ch. Inverness Daphne
1984 Best of Opposite Sex, National Specialty,
Montgomery County Kennel Club
Owned by James and Helen Heintz

Ch. Gemar's Morning Dove
1987 Best of Opposite Sex, Regional Specialty,
Bedlington Terrier Club of Greater Chicago
Owned by Gene McGuire and Gretchen Ochsenschlager

Left to right:
Ch. Winphal's Silver Salute
1988 First Stud Dog winner, owned by Tina Westphal with Ch. Carillon Caption E.O., Ch. Bonny Brook
Lambunctious, Ch. Carillon Mareli Bentley Beans, and Ch. Berkshire's Bonnie Carillon
National Specialty, Montgomery County Kennel Club

Gallery of Winning Bedlington Terriers

Ch. Serendipity Salieri
1988 Best of Breed, Regional Specialty, Bedlington
Terrier Club of Greater Chicago
Owned by Lucy Heyman

Ch. Marvay's Taylor Made
1989 Best of Winners, Regional Specialty,
The Bedlington Terrier Club of the West
Owned by Martha McVay

Ch. Sudor's British Sterling
1991 Winners Dog, National Specialty, Montgomery
County Kennel Club
Owned by Kenneth Russell and Dolores King

Ch. Carillon Platinum To Th'Core
1991 Best of Breed, National Specialty GWTF Silver
Anniversary, and 1995 Veterans class winner,
Louisville National Specialty
Owned by Kharlene Boxenbaum

Gallery of Winning Bedlington Terriers

Left to right:
Ch. Carillon Pure Platinum
1991 First Brood Bitch, with co-owner Kelly Hitchcock and three of her five champion offspring; Ch. Sudor's Crystal, Ch. Sudor's White Linen, and Ch. Sudor's British Sterling
National Specialty, Montgomery County Kennel Club

Ch. Barma's Lady Jane Grey
1992 Winner Bitch, Regional Specialty, Bedlington Terrier Club of Greater Chicago
Owned by Paula Von Gerichten

Ch. Inverness Deirdre
1992 Best of Opposite Sex, National Specialty, Louisville Kennel Club
Owned by James and Helen Heintz

Gallery of Winning Bedlington Terriers

Ch. Sudor's White Linen
1994 Best of Breed, National Specialty, Montgomery County Kennel Club
Handled by Kelli Hitchcock and owned by Kelli and Jeff Hitchcock

A collection of winners from the Stud Dog class at the 1994 National Specialty, Montgomery County
Kennel Club.
From left to right:
Kel-Ti's Sudor She's No Angel with Tina Humphries
Ch. Sweet Briar's Carillon Cody with Deborah Regan
Ch. Sudor's White Linen with Kelli Hitchcock
Ch. Kel-Ti's Maximum Overdrive with Sherry Kotishion

Gallery of Winning Bedlington Terriers

Ch. Carillon Fuzzy Logic
1995 First Stud Dog, National Specialty, Montgomery County Kennel Club
Owned by Lucy Heyman
Shown here with Ch. Fuzzi Logic Cache Controller, handled by her owner Donna Reddiconto,
and Ch. Fuzzi Logic Jil Sander Sudor handled by Barbara Lundy

Ch. Sudor's Magic Noir
1996 Winners Bitch and
Ch. Bonnybrook's Magical Sudor
1996 Best of Winners National Specialty, Montgomery County Kennel Club
Owned by Kristin Dorsey and Dolores King

Gallery of Winning Bedlington Terriers

Ch. EJ's Irish Bramble Bryar
1996 Winners Dog, Regional Specialty, Bedlington
Terrier Club of Greater Chicago
Owned by Paula Von Gerichten

Ch. Gemar's Anything Goes
1996 Best of Breed and Best of Winners, National
Specialty, Minneapolis, Minnesota
Owned by Gene McGuire and Gretchen Ochs

Ch. Valgo's Rock N' Roll
1996 Best in Sweepstakes, Great Western Specialty,
Great Western Terrier Association of Southern
California
Owned by Robin Little and Marjorie Hanson

Meadowsweet Summer's Hot
1998 Best of Winners, National Specialty, Montgomery
County Kennel Club
Owned by Vanessa Sypher

Gallery of Winning Bedlington Terriers

Ch. Silvery Moon Unforgrettable
1998 Best of Breed, National Specialty, Montgomery County Kennel Club, under judge Joe Purkneiser
Owned by Kay and Richard Kraft

Ch. Noel's Tia Gemar
Winners Bitch, BTCGC 1983 Specialty, handled by Fred Bremer
Owned by Gene McGuire

Working with a Bedlington Terrier

⌒⁄⅂⌒

E very Bedlington should be able to lie around the house, have a good meal, receive love and attention, and be taken for a walk or a romp every day. However, some owners like the challenge, bonding, and companionship of working with their dog and training him to follow commands.

⌒⁄⅂⌒

OBEDIENCE

Spectators at a dog show love to watch the obedience rings because they can understand what the dog is doing (or not doing) much better than when they watch the conformation rings. Although most of the basic obedience skills are familiar to average dog owners, the level of training in the show ring is indeed impressive and the teamwork of the dog and handler inspiring.

For obedience work, both dog and handler need aptitude and determination. The handler must take time to work with his dog every day, even if it is only for five minutes or so. The handler must also have patience, and the dog must have a desire to perform and at least some willingness to please. Once this match is made, a handler and his dog can be well on their way toward the obedience degrees. The handler will feel a tremendous amount of achievement and accomplishment to have such a smart little dog working by his side.

Ch. Hollywink Maxwell, CD, CDX, UD, with owner/handler Rita Trish. As of 1997, one of the few Bedlingtons with a Utility degree.

Obedience classes are offered throughout the country, and unless you live in a very remote area, your town or city should offer you a selection of training opportunities. Some classes are offered by private individuals and others are offered by obedience clubs or all-breed clubs. There are different methods of instruction, and you may find it worthwhile to visit various classes to see which method of training you prefer.

You will usually start your pup at about six months of age, and some classes will not take a dog any younger. Classes will meet once or twice a week for six to ten weeks. Having successfully completed one of these classes and passed the examination at the end of the class, you should have a dog that will sit on command, come when called, and walk decently on a lead. This is all that many dog owners require. They want a pet that behaves like a gentleman or a lady. If you have never owned a dog before, or never owned a dog with

Carillon Tyler Blue, CG, CDX, shown winning First Place with a score of 196.0, quite an achievement for a Bedlington Terrier. Owned by Donna Hurley.

good manners, obedience class work may be just what you want and need.

For those who have a genuine interest in obedience, your class work will continue beyond this, and you will start working for degrees and titles, just as you would with a dog in the conformation ring. At this point, if you have not been training with an obedience club, you may want to consider finding one that you can join.

The American Kennel Club offers the following obedience titles: Companion Dog (CD) is earned in Novice Class, Companion Dog Excellent (CDX) is earned in Open Class, and a Utility Dog (UD) degree is earned in the Utility Class.

To earn a degree, the dog must qualify for at least 170 of the 200 points at a trial, and you must win half of the points in each exercise. When a dog has qualified, he has earned a "leg." Three legs under three different judges must be earned before the dog receives his title. Once a title is earned, it becomes a part of the dog's name, just as Ch. (Champion) becomes a part of the name when won in the conformation ring. Obedience titles are added at the end of the name rather than at the beginning.

In an obedience trial, you are competing against yourself. If there are 20 in the class and 10 receive scores of 170 or more, 10 dogs will receive their leg at that show. In conformation showing, you compete against all other dogs because there is only one Best of Breed dog.

Novice Classes consist of heeling on lead, standing for examination, coming when called, the long sit (one minute), and the long down (three minutes). In Open Classes, all work is done off lead, which includes heeling, coming when called, dropping to a down position on command, retrieving a dumbbell, and jumping over the broad jump. In Utility, the exercises become much more complicated and include signals, scent exercises, directed retrieve, and directed jumping. These are ambitious programs requiring great effort and patience on both the handler's and the dog's part.

Jane Hannaford-Brunk's first Bedlington, Olivia, winning her first points. Shown by Helen Heintz with the happy owner looking on.

If you decide to work toward an obedience degree, lessons and class work are essential. Daily practice is also a must. If you become active in an obedience club, you will be aware of the obedience matches that are offered in your area. A match is an opportunity

There are Bedlingtons that have done very well in obedience competition. Janet Brock with her obedient Valgo Bedlington.

for you to work your dog in a show-like setting without paying the fee required for entering an AKC-licensed obedience trial. Entry fees for a match are minimal, and judging will be done by amateurs who have done extensive obedience work. You cannot earn any "legs" at a match, but you will learn how a show works and what will be required of you and your dog.

Although the Bedlington is not a common sight in the obedience ring, there are some Bedlingtons that have done very well. In the 1970s, Fae Johnson had two Bedlingtons that did extremely well in obedience, in spite of the comment of other Bedlington owners who thought that obedience training was a lost cause for a terrier! Fae's Lia Tu Valentine of Bedmor achieved the titles of CD, CDX, and UD as easily as a dog of any other breed. "Lia" loved to track and was out in the field at eight years of age. Fae's Valgo's Sticky Wicket achieved all three obedience degrees before she was two years of age. Fae felt that the older dog was helpful in training the young dog to perform "new tricks."

AGILITY

Agility is a relatively new sport that came to the US from England. The handler and the dog, working as a team, go through a timed obstacle course. Scoring is simple and objective, based on the dog completing all of the obstacles and the speed with which this is accomplished.

In order to compete in this sport, you must belong to an all-breed club or an obedience club where there are individuals who support this event. The obstacle course not only requires substantial space, but the obstacles themselves are fairly large and complex.

Basic obstacles are a seesaw, pipe tunnel, collapsed tunnel, and weave poles. Jumps and hurdles will include the broad jump, tire jump, and high jump. Jumps are at least one times the dog's height at the withers and never more than $1\frac{1}{2}$ times his height.

Many dog shows now hold agility as an exhibition. The ring is usually easy to find, because spectators can be four deep around the entire area. A great deal of enthusiasm emanates from all quarters: cheers from the spectators, barking from the dogs, and loud encouragement from the handlers. This truly is a fun sport.

WORKING
TRIALS

Bedlington Terriers are bred for sport and are one of the gamest of terriers. Even if most Bedlingtons have not been required to use these skills on an everyday basis, the instinct remains in a well-bred Bedlington. All Bedlington owners are familiar with the rapt attention that this dog will give a squirrel that crosses his path, the quickness to find a mouse, or the speed with which he can flush out a rabbit in a field.

The American Working Terrier Association offers Certificates of Gameness at sanctioned trials. Dogs are put through the requirements beginning in the Novice Class. The dog must enter a ten-foot-long tunnel buried in the ground, which will include one right-angle turn. He can take any amount of time to enter the tunnel, but he must reach the prey in one minute and then work the prey for 30 seconds. If he completes these tasks in the required time, with no encouragement other than the command given when he is released to enter the tunnel, he will have qualified in the Novice Class, and will then move up to the Open class.

Bedlingtons can use their natural abilities to excel in working trials. Carillon Shiloh by Starrlite, CD, is shown here qualifying for her Certificate of Gameness awarded by the American Working Terrier Association. Owned by Donna Hurley.

In the Open Class, the tunnel is 30 feet long with a minimum of three right-angle turns. He again must reach the prey in 30 seconds and work the prey for one minute without stopping.

Working trials, like obedience trials, are open to dogs of all ages.

Bedlingtons are bred for sport and are one of the gamest terriers. Carillon Tyler Blue, CG, CDX, shown here on his qualifying run for his Certificate of Gameness. Owned by Donna Hurley.

Again, the sport requires a willingness to compete on the dog's part and the usual patience and perseverance on the owner's part.

JoAnn Frier owned Corborus' Arwen of Aragorn, CD, CG, WC, in the early 1970s. She completed her obedience degree with high scores, but neither dog nor owner were interested in doing more work in obedience. Later in the same year, JoAnn took Arwen for a walk in a field and noticed that she loved to put her head in the ground holes, looking for "something." JoAnn took her to a Working Trial, where she earned her Certificate of Gameness. And at the age of 8¹/₂, Arwen earned her Working Certificate, one of only 15 terriers who had earned this degree at that time.

⌒≈⌒

FLYBALL   Flyball started in California in 1972. Flyball is a relay race of four dogs who race, one at a time, down a 51-foot course with four hurdles set ten feet apart. At the end of the course there is a box that holds a ball. The dog jumps on the box, releases the spring, and the ball flies out. The dog then catches the ball and runs back to the beginning, jumping the hurdles along the way. There are three to five heats and the fastest team wins.

This is a lively sport for dogs and owners. Only two Bedlingtons have flyball titles: Carillon Tyler Blue and his daughter, Topseed Jilly Bean, owned by Lucy Heyman and Donna Hurley.

⌒≈⌒

OTHER ACTIVITIES KNOWN TO BEDLINGTONS   If you are so inclined, there is much that you can do with your Bedlington Terrier to keep you both busy. These anecdotes are just a couple of examples.

Robin, a stray Bedlington found in an animal shelter, was noted for her keen hearing and placed in a Hearing Dog program. After becoming a Certified Hearing Dog, Robin went to live with Dr. Carolyn Shaw Bell, a nationally known economist. Robin travels

Shammy, showing off his newly discovered carting abilities. Owned by Peg Johnston.

with Dr. Bell and makes her life easier in all respects. Both Robin and Dr. Bell are active in the Hearing Dog program. Robin is now 12 years old and growing a bit deaf, and a new Bedlington Hearing Dog, Dustin, will be joining Dr. Bell and Robin to make life a bit easier for both of them.

Peg Johnston noticed that her Shammy seemed "bored" and felt that he needed something to do. Peg had a friend with a Border Terrier who had a little cart that he pulled around the neighborhood. Peg went to the cart maker and had a cart and harness made up for Shammy. The cart was red and had painted Bedlingtons around it, along with a mini-license plate with the name "Shammy" on it. Peg wrote, "Due to my lack of patience, I couldn't wait to get home with the cart and see what Shammy would do with it. I was so excited that he had one second to sniff the harness, one second to walk around the van, and one second to look at the cart as I backed him into the car hitch. He acted as if he had been pulling this $1\frac{1}{2}$ x $2\frac{1}{2}$ foot contraption all of his life. Shammy had found himself!" Shammy soon became a feature at nursing homes, demonstrations, parades, and even at the Cleveland Sportsman's Show.

One other activity that is always special to both dog and owner is taking your pet to a nursing home once a week to visit with the residents. If you like to volunteer and have a mellow dog that likes to be petted, this may be an activity for you. Call some nursing homes or your local animal rescue organization to find out if they sponsor such a program.

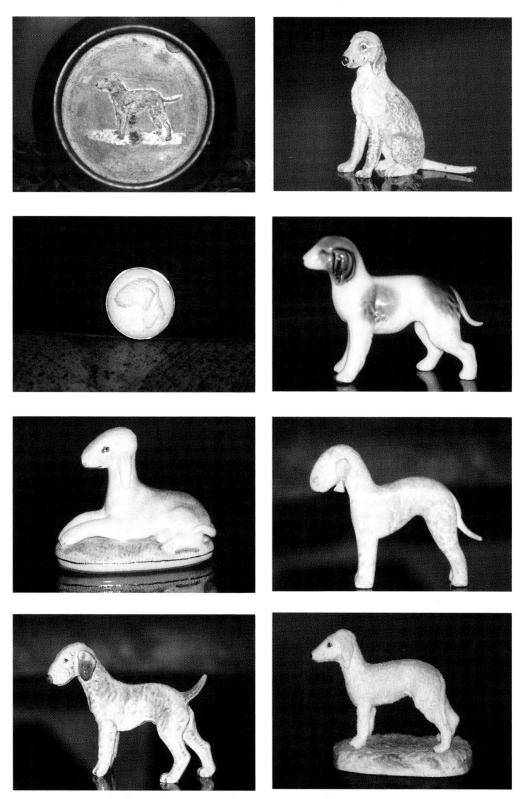

Bedlington Terrier artwork, from the collection of Ralph Hogancamp.

Bedlington artwork from the collection of Anthony Neary.

Epilogue

Considerable research went into the writing of this book, and as the chapters grew in length, I became more aware of the tremendous amount of work that individuals have done, not only for this breed, but for the sport of dogs in general. Without these individuals, the world of dogs would not be the same.

The newcomer often does not realize what makes a breed, a breeder, or a breed club. The breeders who were mentioned in this book did not "make it" in a year, two years, or even five years. It took years of breeding to establish a line, and it took years of being a foot soldier to become well known in the breed. Those who have made it and who have a kennel name that is recognized as producing winning dogs have been the individuals who have stuck with it through the lean years and the good years, through the years of some great winners, and the years when the wins were not so great. Meanwhile, these individuals worked for the breed, belonged to their all-breed clubs, carried the coffee pots to the matches, and stood all day in the rain to be ring steward.

The true dog person is knowledgeable about other breeds and often judges matches for other breed clubs. The true fancier will give his time and often his money to the national club. He will serve on the committees, attend meetings, and do the grubby work that it sometimes seems that no one else wants to do. He will help new individuals with grooming and handling, and he will be pleased when a Bedlington Terrier goes Best in Show, even if it isn't of his own breeding.

The old-timers of the breed, those who have been around for 20, 30, and 40 years, understand this. They have paid their dues and continue to pay them with few complaints. This is what makes a great dog person.

Breed and show your dogs, but also become active in your all-breed club and the Bedlington Terrier Club of America. Learn as much as you can about other breeds and about how a dog show functions. And remember, although you can't learn it in a day and you don't become a star in a year, if you stay with it you will gain knowledge, make friends, and have enough good times to make it all worthwhile.

Index